We
Came
to Kosova

WE
CAME
TO KOSOVA

**Twenty-five years of
evangelical experience**

David M. Young

**Christian Focus Publications
Albanian Evangelical Mission**

© Albanian Evangelical Mission

ISBN 1-85792-595-5

Published in 2000
by

Christian Focus Publications, Geanies House,
Fearn, Tain, Ross-shire
Scotland
IV20 1TW

www.christianfocus.com

Cover design Alister MacInnes
Cover picture Maxhunaj
Map Iain Messider

Printed and bound in Great Britian by
Cox & Wyman, Cardiff Road, Reading

CONTENTS

Then... there begun Nirnaeth Arnoediad,
Unnumbered Tears, for no song or tale can contain
all its grief.

- J. R. R. Tolkien, *The Silmarillion*

* * *

Rwy'n gweld o bell y dydd yn dod,
Bydd pob cyfandir is y rhod
  Yn eiddo Iesu mawr;
A holl ynysoedd maith y môr
Yn cyd-ddyrchafu mawl yr Iôr,
  Dros wyneb daear lawr!

Watkin H. Williams

Chapter 1: THE ROAD TO KOSOVA

The journey on which you go is under the eye of Lord.

- Judges 18:6

It is a long road to Kosova. Nine years long in my case.

But that takes us back to the year 1965, and a small snowy town in Germany. The story is briefly told in the book *Mission Albania*, and may one day be told more fully.

Leaving the first eight of those eventful years as told in the other book, we come to 1973 and take up the story there, following the last year and a half more fully than in *Mission Albania*.

I was living in Groombridge, Sussex, and engaged to my fiancée Margaret Woodger. Eastern Europe was already lurking on the fringe of our lives, and seemed to crop up wherever we turned.

In March we received a letter from my friend Alvis Straupe, of Cambridge days:

> *I myself am at a significant turning-point in my life... I have been invited to participate in this by going to Germany for about two years, primarily to act as administrative assistant for the expanding work in Central, Eastern and Southern Europe. I leave in the near future...*

In October, we visited John MacFarlane, another friend from Cambridge days, recently back from studying in

Prague. He had gone there from Cambridge with a view to doing what he might for the Lord, and it was all very brave and secret, for Czechoslovakia was a dark and dangerous place for Christians to serve their Lord.

I was often more moved by what people did than what they said, and this sort of decisive action tended to make a deep impression upon me. But I was not expecting a full-time work for eastern Europe myself: rather, I was sure God had called me to the ministry in this country. Nonetheless, the principle set forth in Proverbs 16:9 was working itself through: "A man's mind plans his way, but the Lord directs his steps."

On 2nd. July 1973 there was a church meeting at the Strict Baptist chapel in Borough Green, Kent, at which the pastor and members decided to send me out to preach. On 25th. July, I was commended in prayer to the work of the ministry and was soon recommended to the churches. The September 1973 issue of *Grace* accordingly contained this notice:

> *The Church at Borough Green, having listened with profit to the ministry of the Word through Mr. David Young, M.A., recommend him to the Churches.*

I was engaged to preach on forty-four Sundays out of the fifty-two that year, sometimes at three services. Preaching definitely seemed to be the calling God had given me.

But a strange new theme began to appear in what I thought and wrote. On 12th. July I heard Mr. A W Clark preach at the Strict Baptist chapel in Hadlow from Genesis 17, where Abraham's prayer for the prosperity of Ishmael was heard and answered, but the real purpose of

God was to be fulfilled **at this season next year**. I was beginning to feel that July 1974 would be the season when God would give us the longer-term ministry He was planning for us.

We were married at the chapel in Borough Green on 28th. July 1973, and moved into a farm cottage in the village. We soon began the practice of spreading out a map of Europe on the settee on Saturday mornings, kneeling in front of it, and praying for each country of eastern Europe in turn.

In August I was still feeling that God would lead me into a pastorate "or other ministry" the following summer, and the feeling did not leave me. In November it came to the fore again, when my attention was drawn to Deuteronomy 24:5: *When a man is newly married, he shall not... be charged with any business; he shall be free at home one year, to be happy with his wife whom he has taken.* I told Margaret that it seemed to point exactly to July 1974 as the time when God would lead us into our work and ministry. By the end of the year, I was even wondering whether "some kind of missionary involvement" was God's plan for us, rather than a pastorate: "Maybe July, 1974, and after will show us."

About the same time, another couple, Richard and Margaret Worthington, were living in Tonbridge, where Richard was a science teacher. They had attended various conferences, prayed for people they knew travelling to eastern Europe, and supported missions working there, particularly Open Doors, and they were feeling the need to pray regularly with others for that area. They set up a regular prayer meeting and advertised it through Open Doors magazine, then known as *Gateway Outreach*. In response to the advertisement, we wrote to them, and were invited to join the meeting. It met once a month on a Friday evening at their home.

Gradually I came to feel that the whole of eastern Europe plus the Soviet Union was too much to pray for informedly and effectively: I needed to narrow it down, and asked God to guide me. I also felt I needed to learn an eastern European language if I was to be effective on any occasional visits among the people on whom my interest was to be concentrated.

Following my entry into the ministry in July, and whilst waiting for a call to a pastorate, I taught part-time at Wrotham School, a mile or so from the cottage we were renting. One of my subjects was Religious Education, for which no prep. was set, so I had the same number of free periods and lunch breaks as other teachers, and had to remain at the school, but I had a good deal less marking to do. It gave me a fair amount of free time in school, when I had nothing special to do. The study of a new language seemed to be a good use of this spare time. My prayers for guidance regarding which *people* to narrow my interest down to would be answered by the decision which *language* to learn.

I was aware that Albania was the most severe country in eastern Europe, with the harshest restrictions on religion. Before the Second World War it was the only predominantly Moslem country in Europe. After the War, the newly established Communist régime at once began putting limitations on religion, until in 1967 they closed all remaining 2000+ religious buildings and declared themselves the first truly atheistic state in the world. A new Constitution prohibited all religious

4

organisations and activities, and no mosques or churches were open for worship anywhere. Religious people who resisted such oppression suffered appalling persecution.

There was only one Evangelical church in Albania prior to the Communist take-over, and only about a hundred Evangelical believers in the whole country. Their pastor Koci Treska was imprisoned and tortured for his faith; others too were imprisoned; some lost their lives during the War. We had no contact with that church, or with any individual believers in Albania. We did not even know whether the church had survived in any form: it might have managed to continue functioning 'underground', or it might have died out. It might, of course, even have grown under persecution! But nobody knew.

That situation was the background against which I came to sense God's call to take up the challenge of Albania, with the conviction that Albanian was the language God would have me learn, and the Albanians the people He would have me seek to work for.

This sense of divine direction finally crystallised through a conversation on 21st. November: a conversation I have now completely forgotten! I recall neither with whom it was held, nor what we spoke about, and of course I felt the whole matter of Albania was too secret to keep a written note of it. But the same evening, I took the meeting at the chapel and spoke of the need for evangelical broadcasting in Albanian in the context of other needs concerning Albania and its religious situation. Deacon Arthur Hollman felt the Lord telling him that I would learn Albanian to help meet those very needs, but he did not mention it to me. He kept the matter in his heart.

Five days later I shared my sense of leading with the people who met for prayer at the home of one Norman Parker. It was after that meeting that Mr. Hollman told me what he had felt the Wednesday before, and it came to me as an outward confirmation of the inner guidance I had been feeling. It is always a wholesome thing when others of the Lord's people confirm our leadings by their agreement and approval.

In the Christmas holiday, I visited Oxford and went to Blackwell's bookshop, to ask what material they had available for learning Albanian. They pointed me to the correct shelf, and I bought Stuart Mann's *A Short Albanian Grammar*, published in 1932. It was the only book they had on Albanian, and their very last copy: a providential confirmation.

On the last day of 1973 we visited Noel Doubleday, of Open Doors, and he invited us to apply for a training weekend to be held in March, for people planning to travel to eastern Europe for the Lord. The day before we went to the weekend, my reading was in Judges 17 and 18: *Go in peace. The journey on which you go is under the eye of the Lord.* We must have been beginning to think about the possibility of going - or Noel Doubleday might have been thinking it was time we did! Be that as it may, following the interview with him and then the weekend in March, we decided to plan a visit to Kosova. Albania was not open to visitors, and Kosova was the main Albanian-speaking region of Yugoslavia. It was our obvious next step if we were going to develop a ministry for the Albanian people.

A few days later we bought a short-wave radio, and as Margaret fiddled almost idly with the knobs she "happened" to tune in to Radio Tirana's English-language programme just as it was beginning. It was the first programme that we found: another providence.

About the same time we heard of Sali Rahmani, from Ferizaj in Kosova who had turned to Christ whilst in Vienna, and was in Britain to train for Christian work. Something of his story is told in *Mission Albania*. He came to visit us, and we developed contact with him, and indeed have maintained it ever since. In time he became one of the four founders of the Albanian Evangelical Trust (later re-named Mission).

On 25th. April there was a church meeting at the chapel in Hadlow, chaired by Peter White, Secretary of the Strict and Particular Baptist Trust Corporation. Following that meeting, a call to the pastorate at Hadlow was issued. Margaret and I were required to spend part of the meeting in a side room while they talked about us - but the door was not very thick! I had preached at Hadlow a number of times since July 1972, but I had been feeling some disquiet about the possibility of a pastoral call there: I was not entirely sure it was the right place. Nonetheless, I decided that if a call came that was both unanimous and unconditional, I would accept it. It was, and accordingly I did.

It was planned that I would begin the pastorate in September, and the July issue of *Grace* announced that:

> *David M. Young, M.A., has accepted a call to the pastorate of the Church in Hadlow. Induction Meetings will be on Saturday, September 14th (D.V.).*

At the end of the summer term, I left my job at Wrotham School - the last time I was ever to teach in a State school, except for a little supply teaching about thirteen years later.

On Tuesday 23rd. July, Margaret and I set out in our Renault 4 for Kosova. Margaret was pregnant with our first child, Lucy, who was born four months later and joined me seventeen years later on a visit to Albania - something we would hardly have hoped or imagined in those days.

On the first day, Margaret and I travelled as far as St. Dizier, and stayed with Pastor René Kennel, with whom I had worked in evangelism in the summer of 1970. We stopped in Switzerland for a couple of nights, and visited Pastor and Mrs. Willy Droz, with whom I had also worked that summer. In Trieste we stayed with David Borman of the Evangelical Cultural Centre, and enjoyed and benefited from his fellowship and advice.

We used the border and the time of day which he advised when we drove into Yugoslavia, presenting ourselves as convincingly as we could as an ordinary young couple on holiday. What we were taking into Yugoslavia I no longer recall, but whatever it was we were eager not to be too closely searched, and we were relieved and grateful to God that we crossed without difficulty or hindrance. We camped for the night beside the beautiful pine-ringed Plitvice lake in Slovenia. I am not by nature a practical man, and I soon discovered that I had no idea how to erect our tent. A wiser fool would have experimented in his garden before setting off - and would not have made his first attempt to erect the tent atop an anthill! Happily a French couple nearby had a similar tent and were able to come to the rescue. Thus we snuggled into our sleeping bags on two folding camp-beds for our first ever night in eastern Europe.

The journey continued via Sisak, but only because we had been asked to give a lift to a Christian brother - a kindness we regretted, for he was not an easy passenger, and we learnt a lesson which still stands us in good stead - that it is sometimes better to refuse a favour than to ruin or distort a journey, or risk failing to achieve a primary objective. We had to sleep at a house one night, where conditions were cramped and many flies troubled our sleep. (These days I take a fly-swat to the Balkans.)

We took the motorway to Belgrade, drove to Kraljevo, and entered Kosova on the road to Kosovska Mitrovica.

Almost as soon as we were inside Kosova, I stopped the car. Margaret stayed sitting in it, being somewhat frazzled after the lift we had given to our brother, and relieved to be rid of him. I walked up into a field with many colourful wild flowers, and mused that the Albanian people who lived in this region were to be part of the future work God was giving me. There was a real sense of expectation: what would the unfolding years bring as this work developed? I took a photograph of the view, to remind myself for ever of that moment: I still have it.

We visited Prishtinë, Prizren, Deçan and Pejë. At Prizren we camped for the night in the grounds of a hotel where there was a wedding. Albanian weddings are wild, lively affairs, and we were kept awake well into the small hours - and woken up by a cockerel early in the morning. In Deçan we played table tennis with ethnic Albanians who were also holidaying there. A young lady gave me a dictionary as a keepsake, for Albanians will give you whatever they can in token of friendship.

In Pejë we visited Pastor Simo Ralević, of whom more later. It was his home town, and he had planted a Baptist church there some nine years previously. The church building was opened in 1969, and in the same year he began to print books and tracts in Albanian. For many years, he did a noble work, ministering in his small chapel in the Serbian language and continuing his Albanian literature ministry on a grand scale. In fact, it was said to me in 1997 that hardly a home in Kosova had not received his literature. He remained till he was driven out following the conflict in Kosova in 1999.

We then went on to Guci and Ulqin in the ethnically Albanian parts of Montenegro. In Plav, near Guci, we stayed in a hut in the grounds of a hotel, and met a university professor from Chicago, Eric Hamp, and his wife. Prof. Hamp had spent a while in Aberystwyth where he had managed to acquire coal during the miners' strike due to his use of the Welsh tongue; now he was in Montenegro to study the local Albanian dialect. He kindly drew on to my map of Yugoslavia a line defining the extent of the Albanian-speaking area: a map which proved very useful in planning future trips. It was information that was unavailable elsewhere, and our getting it was a divine providence of no small significance.

A remarkable thing had happened shortly before our trip. At the Tonbridge prayer meeting, Richard Worthington said that I would come to a place where I could go no further, and that there God would give me a vision of my future work. While we were at Guci, Margaret went out shopping with Mrs. Hamp, and I set off on a walk along a rough and stony track that leads to Albania. Suddenly, the strap of my sandal broke, and I could literally go no further. I hobbled on to the grassy bank for a time of prayer, and when I looked up I saw in front of me a striking and beautiful view of the Albanian alps, framed in the nearer foothills: a "vision" of the land with which my future work would be so closely interwoven: more closely than I realised at the time.

God had given me the Albanian people as part of my future work, but we did not expect it to be a full-time work: rather, I expected to spend the next four decades or so in preaching and pastoral ministry among the Strict Baptist churches in Britain, continuing an involvement with Albanian work as opportunities came.

As the fourth septennium of my life drew towards its close and I approached the age of 28, we felt we had reached the culmination of 3½ years of determined progress towards that ministry. Life was suffused with promise and joyful hope. The visit to Kosova was soon followed by induction services at Hadlow on Saturday, 14th. September, and pages 13-14 of the November issue of *Grace* carry an account of them which includes this extract:

> *The charge to the pastor was also given by Mr. Obbard. His sermon was based on the words, 'Go in and possess the land which the Lord God of your fathers giveth you' (Deut. 4:1).*

By a remarkable providence the next page, facing that extract, carries an article entitled "Albania in Chains". It was my first published article on Albania: little did I think it would be printed on the page facing those words from Deuteronomy 4: *Go in and possess the land...*!

Following that visit in 1974, I spent more time among Albanians in other places than in Kosova, and went there only briefly.

When the mission was formed in 1986, it was called the Albanian Evangelical Trust (and later re-named Mission, because so many people misunderstood the word "Trust"). We deliberately chose the word *Albanian*, not simply *Albania*, for it was always our aim to bring the Gospel to the Albanian people wherever they were to be found, inside Albania or elsewhere. Kosova was never forgotten, and continued to hold a place in our hearts.

In September 1987 I flew to Tivat, hired a car and drove to Kosova where I linked up with John Quanrud, who was a missionary there, enrolled (for the purpose of acquiring a resident visa) at the University. I stayed two nights at the Kosovski Bozhur Hotel in Prishtinë. I love Kosovar music, and one thing I did while in Prishtinë was buy two cassette tapes from a street vendor to take home with me.

I drove with John to Montenegro with a list of Sali Rahmani's radio listeners to visit. Most of that visit was spent in Montenegro and so does not come into this story.

The music tapes were confiscated by the Yugoslav police at the airport when the time came to fly home. They gave me a receipt, but never returned them.

In October the following year I travelled with a Dutch brother, and our main purpose was to visit listeners to

Sali Rahmani's radio programmes, to ask whether we might answer any questions they had, provide a little new literature, and just show that as Christians we were personally interested and concerned for them.

Our journey took us to Prizren. Arriving at the same time as the returning college students, we were unable to find accommodation anywhere in the town, but Albanian hospitality came into play when we asked help of three young men in the street. They began a door-to-door search for a house where a bed for the night might be found, until eventually one family opened its door and received us. We did sleep in "a bed" - not two - but it was all there was, and we were also welcomed into the family's living room that evening for conversation and Turkish coffee.

We visited Pejë and attempted to see Simo Ralević. I could not remember the way to his home, and the situation for him was already tense enough for us not to feel we could ask people in the street where Rruga Emin Duraku was - that is, the road he lived in. My Dutch companion suggested I attempt to mask our real intention by telling people I had heard what an interesting street it was, and could they tell me how to find it. But I did not follow his suggestion: for one thing, it was untrue; for another, it did not even sound true; and for another, it would quickly have been apparent what the true purpose was of two foreigners searching for the street where Simo lived. We left without finding him.

We headed towards Prishtinë, and attempted to find lodgings on the way as the hour was getting late and darkness had fallen, but we met only with failure and refusal, and were obliged to continue on to Prishtinë, where we put up at the Hotel Kosovski Bozhur. That was my final visit to Kosova in the 1980s.

CARINARNICA — ЦАРИНАРНИЦА **BAR**
CARINARNICA — ЦАРИНАРНИЦА

Ispostava — Испостава
Izpostava — Испостава **AERODROM TIVAT**

Br. — 5р. **1125/7** od — од **26. 09.** 19 **87** god.
St. — 5р. z dne — од год.

POTVRDA — ПОТВРДА
POTRDILO — ПОТВРДА

Na osnovu čl. 354. st. 2 Carinskog zakona ("Sl. list SFRJ", br. 10/76).
Вра основ на членот 354. став 2 од Царинскиот закон ("Службени лист на СФРЈ", бр. 10/76).
Po drugem odstavku 354. člena carinskega zakona ("Ur. list SFRJ", št. 10/76).
На основу чл. 354. ст. 2 Царинског закона ("Сл. лист СФРЈ", бр. 10/76).

Potnik — Патникот **DAVID YOUNG** iz — од **PHOSDDY**
Potnik — Патник is — из

ul. — ул. ____ br. — бр. ____ Obćina — Општина
ul. — ул. št. — бр. Obćina — Општина

koji posjeduje putnu ispravu br. **82. L 31003** izdanu od SUP-a u ____
koj poseduva patna isprava бр. Издадена од СВР во
ki im potni list št. izdan od TNZ v
који поседује путну исправу бр. издату од СУП-а у

dana
na je denot **26. 09.** 19 **87** god.
dne
дана

privremeno je oduzeta do završetka prekršajnog postupka sledeća roba:
привремено се одземена до завршетокот на прекршочната постапка следните стоки:
začasno, do konca postopka o prekršku, odvzeto tele blago:
привремено је одузета до завршетка прекршајног поступка следећа роба:

Red. br. Зад. бр. Zap. št. Ред. бр.	Količina Количина Količina Количина	NAIMENOVANJE I OPIS ROBE — НАИМЕНОВАНИЕ И ОПИС НА СТОКИТЕ IMENVANJE IN OPIS BLAGA — НАИМЕНОВАЊЕ И ОПИС РОБЕ
1	2	Kasete
2	1	FILM SNIMLJENI

Zaključeno za red. br. **2** (**dva**)
Закључено со ред. бр.
Zaključeno z zap. št.
Заључено са реа. бр.

(M. P.) CARINSKI RADNIK ЦАРИНСКИ РАБОТНИК
(M. P.) CARINSKI DE_VEC — ЦАРИНСКИ РАДНИК

Potvrda o privremeno oduzetoj robi ...
Потврда за привремено одземена стока ...
Potrdilo o začasno ...
Потврда о привремено одузетој роби ...

Izdaje: ISCRO "Službena administracija"
OOUR "Službena administracija" — Beograd (6/79)
Štampa: ISCRO "Službena administracija"
OOUR Grafički pogon "Branko Đonović" — Beograd

Chapter 2: Kosova

*There was a little city with few men in it; and a great king
came against it and besieged it.*

- Ecclesiastes 9:14

The Times of 15th. July 1999 describes Kosova as "a
plateau of high, rolling meadows... surrounded on all
sides by jagged peaks... a naturally-fortified pastoral
idyll, studded with Europe's most abundant silver and
lead mines."

To understand the background of hatred and conflict to
life in Kosova we need to look back at least as far as 1346,
when the Serbian Orthodox patriarchate was formed at
the town of Pejë (Peć), and to 1374, when the self-ruling
Serbian church was recognised by the other Orthodox
churches. It made Pejë into the seat of the national
church, and Serbs still regard the region as the *cradle of
Serbia*. Much of the historical information for this small
book is drawn from Noel Malcolm's *Kosovo: a short
history* published in 1998 by Macmillan (London), and all
readers with a serious interest in the long story of Kosova
are advised to make that book the main source of their
study.

In 1389, at a time when Kosova was part of the Serbian
empire, the all-important Battle of the Field of Blackbirds
took place. Without grasping the significance of this
battle, no-one will understand the strife over Kosova
centuries later. A united army of Slavs, Albanians and

Hungarians fought under the leadership of the Serbian Tsar Lazar against the invading Turks. The flower of Serbian aristocracy fell in the battle, including Lazar himself, and the Serbian empire never recovered from the defeat. In the years that followed, the Turkish advance continued, till the final Serbian stronghold fell in 1459.

The battle gave rise to a many poems and legends, and became part of the very heart of the Serbs' understanding of themselves.

In the years following, many Serbs left, emigrating to Bosnia, Dalmatia, Montenegro and Hungary - so many, that in 1483 it was reported that 200,000 Serbs had settled in the south of Hungary in a space of only four years.

In 1691 things seemed to be going badly for the Turks in their various battles, and the Serbs rose against them, but soon fell victim to Turkish reprisals. Another great northward migration of Serbs occurred, and perhaps as many as 40,000 more families settled in Hungary, many of them from Kosova including Pejë the very heart of their religious civilisation.

Albanian Moslems spread north and east into the vacant land. The Treaty of Karlowitz of 1699 concluded the war between the Turks and the Austrians, and put an end to any hope of the Serbs' return.

So Kosova was seen as steeped in Serbian blood and religion, a lost province of their empire. It became Serbia's shrine. It was the heartland of their mediæval culture, and one of the primary aims of the Serbian Orthodox Church was the regaining of Kosova for the Serb nation.

During the 19th. century the Albanian character of "Old Serbia" was increased by further Albanian settlement, which was encouraged after 1878 by the Turkish rulers. At the same time, the myths cherished in the Orthodox Church were taken up by Serbian nationalists. Neither was it an easy time to serve God there, and in 1880 a British and Foreign Bible Society colporteur, Sosnovski, was murdered on a return journey from Prizren.

In her 1909 book *High Albania* the intrepid traveller Edith Durham wrote:

> *Kosovo vilayet was a most important part of the great Servian Empire of the Middle Ages. The Serb of to-day looks at it as part of his birthright, and of its recapture the young men see visions and the old men dream dreams.*

When they re-conquered it in 1912, they felt as if they had returned to their Promised Land. There were scenes of religious fervour - and there was brutality against the Albanian Moslems who lived there. Conflict followed between the Serb "liberators" and the Albanians who were the majority of the population, and the government pursued the now-familiar policy of expelling Albanians and destroying their homes.

It happened like this. Serbia's invasion, supported by their ally Montenegro, began on 16th. October, 1912. A Danish journalist in Skopje reported that five thousand Albanians had been killed in Prishtinë after the city was captured and wrote of a "horrific massacring of the Albanian population". The Roman Catholic archbishop of Skopje, Lazër Mjeda, reported that in Ferizaj only three Moslem Albanians over the age of 15 had been left alive. Gjilan surrendered without a fight, but the population was massacred anyway. Gjakova was completely sacked. Prizren surrendered peacefully, but the conquerors knocked on the doors of Albanian homes, took the men away and shot them, killing four hundred in a few days. The Archbishop estimated that twenty-five thousand Albanians had been killed. The Carnegie Endowment's international commission reported

> *houses and whole villages reduced to ashes, unarmed and innocent populations massacred en masse... with a view to the entire transformation of the ethnic character of regions inhabited exclusively by Albanians.*

A major purpose of all this brutality was to reduce the proportion of Albanians in the province, in an attempt to give some semblance of justification for the incorporation of the conquered territory within Serbia.

After the First World War resistance to Serb domination again flared up. The declaration setting up the new country of *Yugoslavia*, signed in November 1918, gave Yugoslavia territory inhabited by almost half a million Albanians, including Kosova. We need not go into the long sad years of oppression and fear that followed. Suffice it to say that deep-seated hatred and suspicion remained between the Albanians, who were the majority of the native population, and Serbs, in whose hands was all power and who were viewed as an occupying foreign power. They continued their attempts to repress the Albanian population, and to expel as many of them as they could, in pursuance of their dream of rebuilding what they might of their mediæval empire.

In 1944 the puppet prime minister of Serbia together with the leader of the četnik guerrillas offered to fight on the

German side if the Germans would provide them with ammunition and permit them to gather an army of fifty thousand men. They would have had the support of some 90% of the Serbian people. Although things were going so badly by then for the Germans, Adolf Hitler allowed only a very limited experiment, for he did not trust the help they might offer. He said:

The Serbs are the only eternally consistent people in the Balkans. They alone have the strength and the ability to keep pursuing their pan-Serbian aims.[1]

In 1974 President Jozip Broz Tito granted Kosova near-autonomy within Yugoslavia, allowing it to be run by the Albanians. But the grant was not to last long beyond Tito's death.

A report appeared in 1986 in the *Christian Science Monitor* describing Kosova as having the highest unemployment in Yugoslavia, the lowest incomes, and the highest birthrate. There were forty-two applicants for every job, per capita income was 30% of the national average, and living standards were declining rather than improving. Serbian policy had not succeeded in arresting Serbian emigration out of Kosova.

By the 1980s there were something like two million Albanians living in Kosova. The repression intensified after 1989.

In April 1987, the deputy president of the Serbian Party, Slobodan Milošević, was sent to address a group of Serbian and Montenegrin activists in Kosovo Polje, near

---

[1] David Irving, *Hitler's War*, Papermac, London, 1977

Prishtinë. Pre-arranged fighting erupted outside the building between a crowd of Serbs and the police. Milošević cut short the meeting, came outside and uttered his now-famous words: "No-one should dare to beat you!" The crowd were delighted, and Milošević delivered an extemporary speech in defence of the sacred rights of the Serbs. It was the beginning of his rise to fame.

By the end of the year he had become president of the Serbian League of Communists, and he spent a good deal of time and effort the following year in building his power base and influence in Serbia and Montenegro. There were massed rallies, with bussed-in crowds, where the issue was constantly Kosova. But in Kosova mass protests obstructed his progress. In November an estimated crowd of 100,000 resisted his recent plans and moves.

Early in 1989 the Serbian assembly began preparing changes to the constitution which would severely limit Kosova's autonomy within Serbia: Serbia would gain control of the police, courts and civil defence, as well as social, economic and educational policy and the choice of an official language.

New protests followed. Troops were sent into Kosova and a state of emergency declared. Hundreds were arrested. The constitutional amendments were voted through on 28th. March, and Kosova's autonomy was thereby effectively annulled.

On Wednesday 28th. June, at the 600th. anniversary of the Battle of the Field of Blackbirds, Milošević preached his nationalist message to an adoring crowd of a million

Serbs on the meadows of Kosovo Polje. *The Times* called it "the speech which would be the fuse for the explosion of war a decade later" and added that the day "marked Milošević's political coronation as Serb leader".

The second half of 1989 and early 1990 saw further violent clashes with the police, arrests and bloodshed. Twenty-five thousand policemen were transferred to Kosova. In July the Serbian assembly passed a law which made it possible for 80,000 Albanians to be dismissed from their places of work. There was much other abuse of human rights against the Albanian population.

Reviewing this period, the "National Geographic" magazine reported in August, 1990:

> *Serbia had wiped out their autonomy with tanks, troops, tear gas, and terror. Though not many Serbs live in Kosovo, they consider it the sacred heart of medieval Serbia... Slobodan Milošević, President of Serbia, has gone from obscurity to dictatorship, purging party and press along the way, on the strength of one issue - persecution of Serbs in Kosovo... - popularity based not on improving living standards, healthcare, or education but on hammering Albanians and threatening to colonize Kosovo with hundreds of thousands of Serbian settlers... Kenneth Anderson is an investigator with the Helsinki Watch Committee, a human-rights organization that monitors compliance with the 1975 Helsinki accords. His recent report describes the situation in Kosovo as "a frightening example of the power of a one-party dictatorship, the full weight of a police state controlled by one ethnic minority unleashed against another..."*

Chapter 3: In Kosova, 1989-1991

Whom shall I send, and who will go for us?

- Isaiah 6:8

In September 1989 the Mission's first missionary left Britain and settled in Prishtinë, capital of Kosova, where he enrolled as a student of Albanian at the University, thereby gaining his visa to reside in the province and an excellent opportunity to improve both his spoken and literary Albanian.

Mike Brown was born in Manchester in 1960 as the second of five children. His father worked as a research chemist for many years, but later became a school-teacher. His mother was a dressmaker. His parents were religious Anglican churchgoers and he was brought up to go to church and to keep 'The Golden Rule', being good, moral and upright. This gave him a relatively solid foundation and he missed many of the pitfalls that others fall into.

Mike's mother was converted in 1962 in a small Pentecostal mission-hall. After that, he was taken there every now and then instead of to his father's church, but it was not until he was 15 that he went consistently. He felt that everyone there expected him to accept Christ, and he did so and was later baptised, even though he did not feel ready for it. Although he never really doubted after that that Christ was the only way to God and that He could be personally known, there was no deep repentance or extensive Bible teaching in his life. He had not really accepted Christ for himself.

At age 18 he went to University in Liverpool where he studied Mathematics and eventually became joint-top student in Pure Mathematics. His roots in God were still shallow and he attended church only occasionally during those three years. At the end of them he knew he was very empty inside.

After University, he returned to Manchester to live with his parents and for the next six months worked part-time voluntarily in a Christian restaurant and book-shop. It was during this period that God met him in his emptiness and he found Him to be the real satisfier of the heart. He traces his real conversion to this time. Soon afterwards he found work in an insurance firm as a trainee actuary, and later transferred to the computer-programming department.

Although he wanted to follow Christ, he felt there was still something missing in his life, and he began to seek God to satisfy his needs more fully. In a Tuesday night prayer meeting, he had a very real filling with the Holy Spirit that completely turned his life upside-down - an experience which was repeated some three weeks later.

Immediately he not only had a desire to share Christ openly but he found the fear and shame had gone. He got involved in preaching, attended all the open-air meetings that his church organised and took part in the music at the church. He began to lose all interest in worldly success in a career and wanted to live only to work for the Lord.

There was a man in the church, Sam Sharp, who had a burden of prayer for missionary work. Sam held a monthly prayer meeting in the church and Mike attended these. He first got interested in Eastern Europe as they prayed for persecuted Christians in Communist lands and heard testimonies of believers from Western Europe who smuggled Bibles in. Out of all the countries they heard of, Albania seemed to hold a special fascination for him. As we have seen, it was the most closed, allowed no religion whatsoever and no-one seemed to know anything about it. He did not know then that this was the seed of God's call on his life.

One day another man in the church, Stuart Cunliffe, who had been a missionary in Spain and was a man whom Mike respected very much, gave him a book to read, *Rees Howells - Intercessor* by Norman Grubb. Mike took the book to be polite, but did not read it for six months. Then one day Stuart asked him if he had finished it, so he decided he had better read it so that he would not be ashamed when he gave it back.

What he read fascinated him. Here was a man who knew God in a deep way, could get clear guidance, could trust God to meet all his material needs and whose prayers were answered in very real ways. Mike knew that he did not have that depth of reality in his own life, but after reading the book, he began to hunger after something deeper in God.

He began to consider the idea of going to Bible School, and Sam Sharp and others encouraged him in this. His final commitment to apply came as a result of challenges given at the Mission '83 Youth Congress in Lausanne, Switzerland.

He was accepted to start at the Bible College of Wales in September 1983. He did not feel a call to any particular kind of ministry but was simply hungering to know God more. He gave up his job and went to College hoping to learn more about Him.

Bible College, more than anything else, was his 'time in Arabia', a time set apart in which God put Mike's roots down more deeply in Him. He learned to spend much time with God. The Bible became a very precious book. The principles of faith and prayer were instilled into the students. Early on in his first year he felt seriously challenged to step out and trust the Lord to meet all the material and financial needs in his life in answer to faith and prayer, and he learned many lessons about dependency on God which have served as a basis for his ministry since then.

They also prayed much for the Soviet-bloc countries and his interest in Albania began to develop, but still he did not recognise it as a call.

When he finished his course in 1986, he went on a three-week ministry trip to Yugoslavia during which he made his first trip to Kosova and saw Albanian people for the first time. Back in Britain, he returned to Swansea and helped to teach Elementary New Testament Greek to the Bible College students to fill in for a lecturer. When he made his final break with the College in 1987, he decided to make Mount Pleasant Baptist Church, Swansea, his home church.

One of his problems now was that he did not know anyone else who had the same interest that he had in Albania. It was a rare thing in those days! Someone gave him my address, and he felt that it proved to be a divine contact. I was able to put him into contact with all the other major people in Britain who had a similar interest, and he realised that God was finally beginning to confirm his call to Albania.

In Spring 1987, quite out of the blue, he received an invitation to go as a tourist to Albania from a Christian couple whose address I had given him. He was ecstatic! It was a dream come true, for it was still quite rare for Westerners to go to Albania. It meant he had to trust God directly for the money needed because he did not have it, but College had prepared him for such things and God graciously supplied. He was also invited to go on an evangelistic trip in July through Western Europe doing evangelism among ethnic Albanian foreign workers and refugees. This all served as further confirmation on his call.

Thus in September 1987 he went to Albania for the first time. What he saw there during those 2 weeks horrified him - the total control of the secret police, the deafening propaganda, the total denial of even basic human rights, the almost total impossibility of doing evangelism, the people living as slaves in fear of a régime they obviously hated, the poverty... He came back a different person and realised his life was at a cross-roads. He made the most important decision of his life, feeling sure that God was calling him to go there one day as a missionary, and threw himself into preparing for it.

His church did not initially understand or accept his call, partly because they did not yet know him very well and partly because Eastern Europe was still closed, so he had to walk by faith with the support of some close friends.

He began a part-time course at London University studying the Albanian language and spent some hours every day working through a grammar.

During those two years, 1987-1989, confirmation of his call to Albania came repeatedly in different ways: the changes in Eastern Europe generally; continual provision of finances to go on a total of five trips to the Balkans; meeting all the main people in Britain involved in Albania and getting involved in prayer-meetings and conferences with them; continually coming across magazine articles about Albania, sometimes in the strangest of places (once in a Jewish barber's shop on the magazine pile!); confirmation through other believers as they sought God with him; and finally his own church's recognition that "this is of God".

In 1986 he had wanted to go to Yugoslavia straight away after college (as Albania was closed to anyone but tourists) to live among the ethnic Albanians in Kosova as a missionary. But he felt a check in his spirit: it was not the right time and he knew he did not have enough prayer support from others. So he waited in Swansea. It was a frustrating time and he was very unsettled, living in constant tension between knowing he was supposed to stay in Swansea and yet knowing his heart was really in the Balkans. It always took a real effort to commit himself to doing work in Swansea.

However, the period from Spring 1987 to Summer 1989 served as an apprenticeship in ministry. Earning his bread doing part-time tutoring of Muslim school children in order to help learn more about Islam, he also worked alongside the local city mission doing evangelism primarily among Jehovah's Witnesses, the Muslim immigrant community and students, and also in his local church mainly doing Bible Studies with two groups of young people. He went to Albania a couple more times to keep his vision fresh.

Towards the end of 1988 he felt very restless and, while on another ministry trip to Yugoslavia and Greece which also included a trip to Prishtinë, he had a settled conviction that the time had finally come to make the geographical move to Yugoslavia to live among the ethnic Albanians there and begin life as a missionary. His church supported him in his move. He joined the Albanian Evangelical Trust in 1989 as our first missionary among the Albanians.

On Wednesday evening, 2nd. August, Mike's valedictory service was held at Mount Pleasant Baptist Church, Swansea, and I was privileged to preach the sermon. We looked at Onesimus, the idle worker, the thief, the runaway slave who was converted to faith in Jesus Christ and went beyond what even the scriptures required in his commitment to serving his Lord, when at real risk to himself he returned to his master in Colossae. There he became a faithful and trusted brother and a respected Christian worker, a very pattern for our own lives. But he needed the support of a loving church for his life and service. This, I said, was the pattern Mike and his church should aim for in the coming years of his resident service among the Albanian people.

So in the autumn of 1989 Mike went to Prishtinë and began further language study at the University, together with other members of the missionary community. The next two years were mainly concerned with beginning to learn the culture, getting through culture shock (which was heavy!), and speaking Albanian.

He wrote to us:

> *The language is coming slowly and, having made a few gaffes, I've learnt some cultural points, although there's a long way to go; and in recent weeks it has been my privilege to share the gospel with a number of my friends, some of whom have accepted the NT and Psalms. Would you pray with me that... God will water those seeds and bring forth fruit in His time?*

Attendance at the university language and literature course dominated much of Mike's time in Prishtinë. He passed all relevant examinations in June 1991, and gained a fair amount of proficiency in the Albanian language.

He attempted to "sit where they sit", seeking out Albanians, eating and drinking with them, talking about their problems and wishes, befriending them so as to get below the surface of cultural friendliness to the real people. As he began to learn the culture, he had the privilege of making quite a number of friends.

It was a time of trouble, and things were not easy in Prishtinë. Kosova experienced violence, demonstrations and deaths. Mike wrote in February 1990: "There was much bloodshed but everything died down when the army moved in."

Three months later the hearts of all missionaries in Prishtinë missed a few beats when one of them, an American, was stopped at the border and his car searched. Several letters from missionaries to the outside world were confiscated, among them one of Mike's containing comments on the political situation. The risk of exposure of the missionaries' true motives was greatly increased. "Some other folk's letters," Mike wrote, "were hot enough to melt lead on and there's no way now that they do not know our activities."

He decided to write all future letters inside Greece, but his precautions did not prevent his name being given in a book written by Marko Lopushina and published in Belgrade in 1997 by the Alpha publishing house under the title *Kill Your Neighbour*. In 1996 a false brother went to the press and gave "information" which led to allegations that the missionaries associated with the church had been foreign spies. The book was about people who, in the period 1946 to 1997, worked against the interests and security of Yugoslavia in collaboration with various agencies including the CIA. Others named were Sali Rahmani, one of the founders of this mission, Anton Krasniqi (the pastor in Prishtinë) and Simo Ralević.

In May 1990 Mike wrote:

It's much on my heart to work with close links with Anton's church. I believe God wants to establish that church as a strong base. Pray for closer relationships with those concerned.

In July 1990 I flew out to spend a fortnight with Mike, meeting him first in Thessalonica. The visit did not begin too well. The receptionist at the Hotel Argo in Thessalonica refused to let me into the room which had been booked, and I had to wait on the street till nearly 4.30 a.m. when the receptionist came and admitted me.

As he spoke no English, and at that time I spoke no Greek, no clear explanation was communicated. But as the days unfolded, there were significant and valuable personal contacts and opportunities for witness, fellowship and prayer.

After spending a time among Kosovars and Arvanites in Greece, we took the train back to Prishtinë and spent a few days in Kosova. We visited the beautiful Gorge of Rugova, where the ancient Serbian patriarchal church stands just outside Pejë, and also visited Simo Ralević at his home in the same town.

Mike returned with me to Greece, to take a holiday, but we were not allowed to enjoy the train journey, as Serbs were occupying two or three seats each and refused to allow passengers joining the train to sit down. This was their usual practice. So we stood in the corridor as far as the border at Gevgelija, when Greek officials made the Serbs use only one seat each - and kept some of them waiting so long to check their papers that they missed the train when it continued on into Greece.

During Mike's second year in Prishtinë he felt that one priority was the production of a discipleship course in Albanian, which took the form of a dozen or so basic Bible studies for the new believers in the church there and was completed by October 1990. He was asked to teach the course on Sunday afternoons. Circumstances forbade the completion of the teaching, but the studies were put on to tape, making about seven hours of teaching which was used by new believers in Montenegro, Kosova, Greece and ultimately Albania.

Mike also paid frequent visits to Albanian friends in Tuz, Montenegro, for encouragement, ministry to believers and evangelism; spent time doing outreach among Albanian refugees in Greece; paid two visits to Albania; and spent a week doing practical work on the building of a new church in Skopje. He also made a trip to Vojvodina in northern Serbia for a week of Bible ministry to believers among the Slovak minority.

Another missionary joined the community in Prishtinë in Mike's second year - Shirley Klippenstein. She later joined AEM.

Shirley was born in Winnipeg and brought up on a dairy and grain farm in Randolph, Manitoba. Her parents are both believers. Shirley was baptised at the age of 17 and became a member of the Chortitzer Mennonite Conference, to which her home church belonged - an evangelical conference, with Anabaptist roots.

After High School, she attended Prairie Bible Institute in Three Hills, Alberta, for four years, during which time her call to missionary service became clear, although she had felt the Lord's call in that direction even when she was 13.

Following graduation from Prairie, Shirley spent a while in secular work, until in 1983 she went to work at the Eastern Europe office of the European Christian Mission in Vienna. Several years later, whilst she was working at the ECM office in Northampton, the Lord made it very clear that her long-term ministry would be in church-planting.

Since the beginning of her service with ECM she was involved in various ways in outreach to Albanians, primarily with computer work for the Albanian radio team. God burdened her to pray for Albania, and as the years passed she became increasingly convinced of the need for committed workers in ministries to Albanian-speaking people. Albania and Kosova were very much on her heart, and she spent a good part of 1989 and 1990 waiting on God to direct concerning her next step.

Her awareness of the need for workers among Albanian-speakers moved her to take part in the Albanian Discipleship Camp in Greece in the summers on 1989 and 1990.

She was both challenged and encouraged in a very special way as she spent her first two weeks in Europe at the 1989 camp. It was a couple of days late starting due to visa problems for those coming from Kosova, and Shirley noted that the situation continued to be very difficult for Albanian people living in Kosova. She felt it was a special privilege to get to know Kosovars, and after those two weeks in the Albanian camp, she knew where God wanted her in the future.

Following the camp she went to Yugoslavia to spend time with Albanian friends. She stayed with an Albanian family for three weeks, spending most of the time spent in Prishtinë. She also visited Pejë and Prizren. "It was very difficult for me to leave," she wrote.

She returned to Canada and took a course in Islamic studies at Winnipeg Bible College. She became increasingly aware that "working with Muslims requires much time and patience as you cultivate a friendship and earn their trust".

On 11th. July 1990 she arrived in Greece for the Albanian camp that was held from the 15th. to the 30th., and drew eleven adults and two children from Kosova.

Shirley then moved to Prishtinë to begin serious study of the Albanian language, and to become involved in the work of the Gospel among the people. She enrolled at the University, and found accommodation in the house of an Albanian family with four children, where she enjoyed having her own room and cooking facilities.

During the first weeks she struggled with fatigue and headaches, but before the end of the year was able to write, "I am making many friends who are a very practical help with Albanian."

On Friday and Saturday, the 9th. and 10th. of November, there were two concerts in a public hall with a group from Holland. The church obtained permission to put up posters in public places, and to print and give out invitations. The hall was nearly full both evenings, and many heard the gospel through song and testimony. An invitation was given to come to the church on the next morning, Sunday 11th., and the members and missionaries were delighted to see the church full, with standing room only for those who came last. Anton spoke on: "Who is Jesus Christ?" and many responded to the message after the service.

Shirley wrote, "We thank the Lord for this breath of God's Spirit blowing in Kosovo." By December there were many people coming to the church on Thursdays and Sundays, and Shirley noted a great need for teaching in the basic doctrines and truths of the Bible, especially for those coming out of Muslim backgrounds.

In April 1991 she wrote: "God continues to work in Kosovo. Opportunities for witness and speaking of God are tremendous... so many people are now coming to the church. At this point in time, holding Christian meetings is one of the only permitted activities in the Albanian language because all radio and television in Albanian has been closed down by the Serbian government... Saturdays are very busy for us as there are two meetings that take place. There is a meeting from 12:00 to 2:00 for children and teenagers. These alternate so there are two children's meetings and two meetings for teenagers per month. Also, there is a youth meeting each Saturday evening at 7:00. The response to this meeting has been overwhelming. Those coming are mainly in their twenties and attending the university. About eighty people came that first evening. The ladies' meetings on Fridays are going very well with women coming to the Lord."

But the missionaries' main purpose in being in Kosova was to learn the Albanian language and culture prior to their future ministry in Albania. So when Albania finally opened up in 1991 their next step seemed obvious - a move toward the destinies they had been being preparing for for so long. Including Mike and Shirley, they quietly packed their bags and left Yugoslavia for Albania.

Chapter 4: Yugoslavia, 1991-1998

They covet fields, and seize them; and houses, and take them away; they oppress a man and his house, a man and his inheritance... and build Jerusalem with wrong.

- Micah 2:2; 3:10

Civil war broke out in Yugoslavia in the summer of 1991.

The risk developed that this Balkan War would spread. A possible scenario was as follows. Having achieved their ends in Bosnia, the Serbs, hungry for *Lebensraum* and ambitious to create a larger and stronger *großserbisches Reich*, as one might say, turn their attention more openly and violently to the oppressed province of Kosova. The Serbs were already strengthening their tyranny in Kosova, evicting Albanian families and replacing them with Serb settlers, and attempting to crush Albanian culture by the closure of institutions, although the population was 90% Albanian.

It was reported in 1995 that twenty-two elementary schools and all secondary schools with lessons held in Albanian had been forced to operate in private homes and other makeshift venues as the Serbian régime prevented pupils and staff from entering educational premises, many of which remained virtually empty. This alternate Albanian educational system became a huge challenge to Belgrade's repression of the Albanian population's cultural aspirations.

It was also reported that Kosova had become Europe's most dangerous region for epidemics, following the shutting down of its health system. Lice, ticks, abdominal typhus, meningitis and hæmorrhage fever in the same family as ebola were all reported.

Meanwhile, Serbia stepped up its moves to settle Serbs from Croatia, Knin and Krajina, aiming to colonise Kosova and alter its ethnic composition. Some eight thousand refugees had been settled in Kosova, in addition to four thousand who had come earlier: one thousand in both Pejë and Prishtinë, and one thousand three hundred in the Prizren area, where at the printing company R. Sadiku, fifteen colonists were offered jobs the day after Albanian staff had been dismissed.

So the scenario for the possible spread of the war continues: the Kosovars rise; and the ¾-million Albanians in the Republic of Macedonia rise in support of them. Then the Slav Macedonians fight against their own Albanians, and with a twofold onslaught on their kin, Albania enters the war. Greece already detested Macedonia, and Bulgaria desires some of its territory: so they become involved in the fighting with a view to partitioning Macedonia.

Greece also has inflammatory extremists who wish to annex southern Albania, pretending there is a large Greek minority there by the mendacious ruse of calling all who profess the Orthodox religion Greek. They call part of southern Albania "Northern Epirus". George Papandreou told the Greek parliament on 12th. June 1960 that:

the Greek Governments should know that there is a Northern

Epirus issue. And what is eternally forbidden is the renunciation of the sacred cause. Our claim on Northern Epirus is holy and unremitting.

So Greece takes the opportunity of invading the south of Albania to 'protect' their fellow Greeks. Turkey also enters the war in support of its Moslem Albanian brothers. With Greece and Turkey both involved, there are now two NATO countries fighting in the same war but on opposing sides. And as NATO becomes drawn in, so also might Russia. A scenario for a major conflict.

Serbian ambitions in Kosova were a dire threat to wider peace, and could not be expected to do other than cause resentment, hatred and bloodshed. One reader of our Newsletter wrote to us:

Were not the Balkans referred to as the cockpit of Europe, an allusion to the fact that there was always fighting going on there? Nevertheless, in the midst of it all, the Lord God omnipotent still reigns, and in Psalm 46 we are told that he as part of that universal sovereign sway makes wars to cease unto the ends of the earth. Man's rapaciousness starts them, God's purpose stops them. He restrains the remainder of man's wrath that is not conducive to His praise.

According to the BBC Monitoring Service, the Tirana newspaper *Rilindja* of 3rd. August 1996 carried a report on a news conference held in Prishtinë with Ibrahim Rugova, President of the self-declared Republic of Kosova. The report was published under the title "The US Congress resolution supports self-determination for Kosova." Dr Rugova began the conference by welcoming the US Congress resolution on Kosova, which asked for an improvement of the situation, self-determination and the appointment of a special US envoy for Kosova.

Dr. Rugova also welcomed the stand taken by Secretary of State Warren Christopher in front of the Congress's Foreign Relations Committee, according to which "the Albanians must manage Kosova".

One of our missionaries described the situation thus:

Although 90% of the population, the Albanians are ruled in brutal apartheid style by the ethnic Serbs..., tapping into the Serbian sentiment that the Albanians are outsiders on Serbian sacred ground... According to a new report by Human Rights Watch, police detain or beat up dozens of Albanians every day. Security forces have killed 21 Albanians in the last two years. Ethnic Serbs, especially war refugees, are encouraged to go to Kosovo and take jobs from Albanians.

Kosova Communication reported that an Albanian teacher from Prishtinë, Feriz Blakçori, died on 10th. December 1996 in Prishtinë hospital after being tortured in a Serbian police station. The Blakçori home had been raided the previous day by some forty Serb police in connection with an arms search.

The European Union commissioner for foreign relations, Hans van den Broek, told the Yugoslav foreign minister in Brussels that the normalisation of relations between the European Union and the Federal Republic of Yugoslavia (i.e. Serbia and Montenegro) *cannot be dissociated from the Kosova issue*. In the run-up to the Bosnian peace conference in London in December, sixteen British members of parliament appended a motion on Kosova, expressing regret that the Kosova issue would not appear on the agenda.

It was reported in January 1997 that an Albanian resident of Mitrovica died as a result of severe Serbian police torture which he had undergone towards the end of 1996. Another, from Gjakovë, had one leg and three teeth broken following police torture.

In February the Council of Foreign Ministers of the European Union "indicated its concern about the situation in Kosovo".

In April the United Nations Commission on Human Rights adopted a resolution demanding from the Belgrade régime the ending of torture and ill-treatment of persons in detention and of the repression of the Albanian population. Later in April it was nonetheless reported that two Serbian policemen arrested an Albanian in Komoran and later transferred him to the authorities in Prishtinë where he was subjected to severe physical torture.

In May it was reported from Podujeva that the police had beaten an Albanian and left him with multiple injuries. Later in May the Prishtinë-based daily *Bujku* reported that the Albanian inmates at Dubrava prison had been subject to constant torture by the warders and counsellors. In Pejë two forest warders witnessed the beating to unconsciousness of an Albanian by two policemen.

In June the United States expressed concern over "irregularities" during the trial of twenty ethnic Albanians in Prishtinë. Acting US State Department spokesman John Dinger stated that the trial was *marred by a number of judicial irregularities*.

In March 1997 *The Times* printed an article by T. G. Ash describing Kosova as **a province waiting to erupt**. He described it as "dusty, battered and depressed" and as "traditionally regarded by Serbs as the mystical heartland of their national identity, their "Jerusalem"". The article concludes:

> I left with a horrible feeling that here, too, the lines may be drawn first in blood. And the Yugoslav tragedy that began in Kosovo may yet end in Kosovo.

In October 1997 Dr. Ibrahim Rugova condemned in the strongest terms the Serb riot police crack-down on peaceful protesters. The deputy spokesman of the United States State Department, James Foley, released a statement that "the United States notes with concern the shooting to death at the hands of police of a Kosovar Albanian on October 16."

In November France and Germany jointly called on the president of the Federal Republic of Yugoslavia to open talks on a special status for Kosova. On 19th. November, Serbian police in Deçan organised a massive confiscation of merchandise and currency: every citizen stopped had money seized.

In December Koffi Annan, UN General Secretary, presented the General Assembly with a report on the situation in Kosova, concluding that the Serbian government was violating human rights in all aspects. The UN General Assembly adopted a resolution, calling for the start of a dialogue between Yugoslavia (Serbia-Montenegro) and the leadership of the Albanian people of Kosova. The resolution expressed deep concern over the drastic human rights violations and the repression of the Albanian population. A communiqué from the foreign ministers of sixteen NATO member countries expressed concern over escalating tensions in Kosova.

Chapter 5: the church's isolation

Woe to him who is alone when he falls.

- Ecclesiastes 4:10

The church in Prishtinë came together from about 1980, when an elderly Serbian Methodist lady, two Albanians and some foreigners were meeting together for worship in private homes. Evangelism was done, the church building was opened in 1985, and Anton Krasniqi, an Albanian from a Roman Catholic background, was appointed pastor in 1988. From the late 1980s, various western missionaries enrolled in the university there and worked with the church, including of course Mike Brown and Shirley Klippenstein in 1989 and 1990.

In 1991 the church became isolated on every hand, and Anton Krasniqi felt as if they had undergone an amputation. The church-planting evangelism done in the 1980s which led to the formation of the church had been undertaken by believers from Croatia, and from 1991 Croatia and Serbia were at war: contact with the mother church was lost. In the same month as the war began, Albania opened to the Gospel after fifty-one years of isolation, and all the missionaries left for Albania - except one mission, whose activities were said by Anton to have led to a split in the church! Other believers in Serbia had almost nothing to do with the work, because it is Albanian.

We got occasional phone calls from Anton Krasniqi requesting further supply of literature, but even a single book mailed to Kosova came back with this label stuck over the address: "Due to international sanctions against Serbia and Montenegro we are not able to forward your packet."

We had no direct contact with the Lord's work among the Albanians in Kosova, but our contacts nearby were exploring the best possible way to supply the believers with helpful literature to strengthen and sustain them in their faith and walk with God in those dark times.

In the first half of 1993 a leader of the new church in Prizren wrote to us:

With all respect we decided to apply to you and ask for help. This is a new-born church, from the mother church in Prishtina, and we are facing lots of difficulties. We would appreciate it very much if you would help us with your prayer and Christian books. Thank you, and God bless you.

This letter was printed in our Newsletter, and a reader responded by offering to take some literature for us on a trip to the Balkans. He arrived at Anton's house on the morning of 12th. June, 1993, and was warmly welcomed. Anton was "most pleased" with the literature. After coffee, the visitor slept in the church for most of the day, having slept hardly at all for three days. He remained for the weekend, and found Anton and his wife Donika very hospitable: there was a good deal of fun and laughter, and time spent playing with Anton's two young children, Ylli and Besa.

He also reported that the Albanian believers in Kosova found themselves under suspicion from their fellow

Albanians as a threat to national unity, as a source of division in the Albanian culture and as possible colluders with the Serbs; whilst the Serbs were suspicious of them anyway, because they were Albanian.

In July 1993 Paul Troon, Andrew Fowler, Alison Smith and I delivered a load of literature to Macedonia for onward passage to Anton Krasniqi, through their own local channels. There were also originals for printing literature in Serbia, but sadly this was not put into effect at that time. Nonetheless, all the literature reached the Christians in Kosova, and the letter from the missionary who wrote telling us also said:

> *I would ask you to pray for the Church especially at this time. I believe the Lord is trying to bring them to the place of trusting in Him, a learning process of trusting in a God who can meet every need and who cannot fail. Trust needs to be learnt now as more difficult days lie ahead.*

In 1996 we received this letter from Kosova:

> *I heard about your work for God in Albania, working with Christian literature in their language, and helping spiritual growth of young Christians there.*
>
> *May God bless you as people are blessed through your work.*
>
> *We in Kosova lack Christian literature, we don't have nearly nothing, because now for now it's impossible to get books (even the Bibles) from Albania here - because of the political situation in the region. Also all Christian organisations and missions who work with Albanians have focus their work only in Albania.*

This makes us feel like we are betrayed and left on our ownes.

Since we need Christian literature in our language (Albanian) I ask you to send us at least a copy from each of your publishing, so I can share with others and read all together.

I thank you for understanding and helping us in this way.

We responded, enclosing a small amount of literature and giving the name of a man through whom he might acquire our literature in Macedonia, as and when we managed to get it there ourselves.

A number of people approached AEM during 1996 and expressed concern about the needs in the predominantly Albanian regions of former Yugoslavia, and we were thinking, praying and discussing about what steps we could and should take.

On Thursday, 17th. October 1996, Anton Krasniqi came by bus from Kosova and met my fellow travellers Reinhard Huland and Anthony Matthew and me at the Baptist Church in Skopje. His financial support had dropped seriously and he looked very down-at-heel. Our main purpose was to discuss how we could best supply the Albanian believers in Kosova regularly with literature. We spent about seven hours with him, and I felt we were on the track of a system for regular supply.

There were gospel works in Albanian in five places; in one place six hundred people had recently turned up to an evangelistic meeting. The believers experienced difficulties from a range of directions: the Serbian press; the Albanian press; the Moslems; as well as the threat to their livelihood and security from Serbian colonists.

Darkness also arose within the church of Christ, and we were saddened to learn of the first lesbian wedding 'solemnised' in Serbia. One of those so 'married' was an English woman; the other an Albanian Kosovar woman, prominent in the 1991 evangelism in Tirana and involved with establishing five churches in Albania. She subsequently left the preaching ministry, and worked for a feminist movement.

We remained burdened for the Albanians of Kosova, but how could we help them? A letter sent to Kosova was returned with a local Kosova postmark: obviously it reached the right town, but the post office decided not to deliver it. You might have to try five times to get through on the phone, and when you did, even if the person you wanted was not out, the line could be crackly and might be cut off.

Chapter 6: Again to Kosova

It came into his heart to visit his brethren.

- Acts 7:23

In May 1997 I visited Kosova again. What a difference I found from my first visit of 1974! I travelled from Skopje in the Republic of Macedonia to the border in the car of a German brother, Reinhard Huland, with whom we have much to do, and who kept a vehicle permanently in Macedonia; with us was one of AEM's missionaries, Alison Smith, who was living among the 100,000 or more Albanians of Skopje. Reinhard was unsuccessful in his application for a visa to enter Serbia, as he did not have the right stamp on his papers, but Alison and I had got ours at the embassies in Skopje and London respectively, and we travelled from the border by bus to Prishtinë, accompanied by Anton Krasniqi, who had come to Skopje to meet us.

He and I were able to have serious conversations and prayer - as well as enjoying one another's company, good food, and fun for several days. Their personal and church life was continuing amidst many problems. Accusations against him appeared in the press for imagined offences which could lead to five years' imprisonment. Unrepeatably vile and blasphemous graffiti appeared on the church wall, and government hostility was fuelled by their confusion of the church with such dangerous extremist sects as had recently been reported in the western media.

I preached at the morning service on the Sunday to a small congregation of about ten, including two Serbs; there was an atmosphere of fellowship, sincerity and prayer.

In the afternoon Anton took us by taxi to the monument at the Field of Blackbirds, commemorating the battle there in 1389. We climbed the stone tower; it bears this curse: "Whoever is Serb and born of Serbs that dare not shed blood for Kosovo, let nothing be born from his hand, let him be without son or daughter, without white wine or bread, and may his descendants be cursed for ever."

In the evening, we visited the Roman Catholic priest in the town, Nosh Gjolaj, an Albanian from Montenegro, who had our literature in his church library, and Fehmi Cakolli, pastor of another Evangelical church in Prishtinë.

A couple of days later we visited the home of one of Anton's congregation, which seemed to be the damp adapted basement of a block of flats. Xhemail was unemployed, his wife is crippled, they have six children. They are a gypsy family.

On the Monday, after registering with the police as Anton's guests, we took the bus to Pejë and visited Simo Ralević. He too was continuing his life and service amidst ongoing difficulties. Not long before, for example, a visitor planted a briefcase containing gold and silver in his house, and immediately following the visitor's departure the police turned up for a house search and accused Simo of dealing in smuggled goods. Off he went to prison. Again, a piece of his literature was found in the pocket of someone who committed suicide, and Simo's religion was blamed for the death (though it was rumoured that the "suicide" was hiding in a monastery!). Harassment continued, including the planting of an obvious spy in his congregation to take notes and deter visitors and worshippers. He also came under severe attack in the secular press from the Orthodox priest.

The visit was probably good for my pride, for it became apparent that my earlier visits had left no impression whatever on his mind, even though they held such significance for me: he had no recollection of meeting me before. Nonetheless, it was good to renew face-to-face contact. He was very enthusiastic about the literature we print, especially the translations of Grace Baptist publications, and wanted to see it published in Albanian in Serbia, which would have enabled it to be given away or sold without hindrance. "God brought you here," he said.

Back home in Prishtinë we talked and prayed among other things about the serious medical need Anton's son had and the grave difficulties of getting a safe operation in Kosova at the time. What was he to do? And - just a little annoyance amidst all the other problems - someone had stolen clothes from the washing line whilst we were out.

On the Tuesday, we visited the town of Prizren, where a congregation of about thirty was being led by a young man, Besim Kryeziu, who grew up as a Moslem. He made strenuous efforts to fulfil the duties of his religion, but always felt spiritually empty until he was brought to Christ. The church in the town began about five years before, but had no building of its own and experienced ongoing problems with finding a suitable place to rent, and purchase is very expensive.

The journey by bus back to Skopje on our final day was enlivened by a woman who had been beaten up by the police in Ferizaj. Her mind was disturbed, and she marched up and down the aisle in the bus delivering speeches. Eventually she latched on to me - as such people often seem to - but she was a poor, harmless soul suffering more intensely what so many Albanians felt, that they lived under the régime of a pitiless foreign occupier.

As the bus pulled out of Prizren on the Tuesday, the driver put on some sad, heavy music, presumably Serbian as it was the Belgrade bus, and it well answered my own mood, for this was the beginning of the long journey back home to Wrexham. A different kind of highlight to the visit, the day before I caught the train to come home via Greece, was a walk on the hillside outside Skopje, overlooking the town with its gleaming minarets, lush valley and surrounding mountains: glorious views, warm sunshine, a bag of sweet fresh strawberries, and poignant new memories of Kosova.

We had come to Macedonia from a background of gunfire and grenades in Albania. The bus we were on had been stopped by armed highwaymen and robbed. We reached the border in a van only because the Romanian army, there with the multi-national force, had agreed to escort us with an armoured car bristling with guns, a jeep, a second armoured car and about a dozen soldiers dressed for battle.

Now, having come to Kosova we had been admitted, as it were, right into people's lives. They had pressed us with warmth and affection with requests such as:

> Come and visit us at home.
> Can I have a private talk, please?
> Will you pray with me?
> How soon can you come to Kosova again?

And when I waited at the train station in Skopje for the train back to Greece and the airport, I read a book which begins each chapter with a quotation. Here is one I read while waiting:

> Leave to see and leave to wonder,
> Absence sure will help, if I
> Can learn how myself to sunder
> From what in my heart doth lie.

My heart was torn: I did not want to leave. The needs and the hunger for God's Word and for fellowship were compelling. "Nobody visits us now," said Anton. But God has filled my hands (I believe) with work to do in Britain. My prayer could well have been expressed in the words of Exodus 4:13, though in a different spirit from that of the one who originally prayed them: *Oh, my Lord, send, I pray, some other person.* Maybe the writing and reading of this book will contribute to the answering of that prayer.

Chapter 7: The Cleansing of Kosova

Fire devours before them, and behind them a flame burns.

- Joel 2:3

In the summer of 1997 a spokesman for the Kosova Liberation Army said that the KLA had recently assassinated several Serbian policemen. The KLA was dubbed a terrorist organisation, but as far as I know they never planted bombs in Belgrade supermarkets, captured innocent hostages or murdered Serbian civilians at random, but rather selected uniformed officers of the Serbian régime inside Kosova, who were perceived as legitimate targets as official representatives of an oppressing race.

The first shots of the civil war which erupted in Kosova in 1998 might be said to have been fired on the last day of February in the part of Kosova known as Drenica, in the villages of Qirez and Likoshani, when Serb police killed twenty-four Albanians. They blamed the outbreak of violence on the Kosova Liberation Army who killed two policemen in an ambush. A week later the death toll was eighty-three, including twenty-three women and children.

On Monday, 16th. March, I went to the Yugoslavian embassy in Skopje with the correct documentation to request a visa for Kosova again. I planned to visit two or three pastors, plus others who had written asking for a supply of AEM's literature. As required by Serbian formalities, Anton Krasniqi had gone to the trouble of going to a judge to get his invitation to me officially stamped. But the embassy refused to issue a visa: no reason was given, but one assumes it was the incipient war.

I am often regarded as a somewhat unemotional man, but the embassy's refusal to grant the visa that would have admitted me to visit my friends and brethren pushed me almost to tears. Indeed, I asked myself whether the water in my eyes was really due only to the biting Macedonian wind.

It may be asked why I wished to go - other than to ensure that our literature should get into as many Albanians' hands as possible. I am not the best preacher in North-East Wales, nor the wisest counsellor, nor the strongest man of prayer. What could I offer? Well, I could preach (in Albanian), and listen, and pray. But most of all, when the Serb guns were pounding their villages, their culture was being assailed, and their dead lying unburied in the roads, I just wanted to **be with them** and let them know that they were loved, held in our hearts, not forgotten:

I saw all the oppressions that are practised under the sun. And behold, the tears of the oppressed, and they had no one to comfort them! On the side of their oppressors there was power, and there was no one to comfort them. - Ecclesiastes 4:1-2

I wanted to be that comforter. Maybe someone will ask: "But what of your wife? What if you were shot or detained?" I phoned her before going to the embassy, and secured her full agreement to the risks. "A good wife who can find? She is far more precious than jewels." I record my gratitude to God and to her for her willingness to risk coping without me, if things had turned out differently. Her boss concluded I am either a gun-runner or mad: I am neither. But I hope that the love of God resides in my heart for the Albanians who were living in *fear and loathing under the gun*, to quote the title of an article which appeared in *The Independent* on 3rd. April 1998. The article said:

> the desolate, Serb-ruled province of Kosovo is a place of malign surrealism... lunacy eventually becomes a form of normality... a tiny minority rules over the huge majority.

Reinhard Huland, who (being German) found it easy enough to get a visa for Kosova, went in May. He visited our contacts in two towns, and they both said how heartened they were to receive a visit in those difficult times. The road to Prizren was too dangerous for a visit, as gunmen would shoot at any passing vehicle. He travelled in convoy with other vehicles, and heard much gunfire and exploding of grenades in the background. Police checks of vehicles were thorough, not like the brief, courteous affairs in Albania and Greece; sometimes they simply closed the road. At the end he was unable to leave the country on the day he had planned, as the road to Macedonia was closed.

I decided to try again myself in July, at two different embassies. But the violence continued, and the killing. Could AEM really afford to pay for an air fare to Thessalonica, and a train to Skopje, and a bus to the border, when funds were parlous and the likelihood of being refused a visa again so strong in view of the ongoing turbulence? The aeroplane had to be paid for in advance: the risk of spending money fruitlessly was too great: again, reluctantly, I did not go.

Here are some extracts from letters we received around that time:

> *The Kosova situation is horrible already... Another 'Bosnia' would engulf a huge area... Pray much for the few believers in Kosova - 2.6.98*

> *Bad news from Kosovo! Refugees are pouring over the NE border at Tropoja. I hope the international community at large and God in His sovereign mercy will act to end this Serbian madness. - 10.6.98*

> *What will come out of the situation in Kosovo, only the Lord knows for sure. We can only pray that in some way it will turn out for the furtherance of the Gospel. As a nation, the Serbs seem to have an irrepressible urge to oppress other races. - 19.6.98*

> *Our hearts go out to you and our brethren and sisters especially now in Kosova. How wicked men can be! - 24.6.98*

> *Those who drew the map at the end of the First World War probably had no real idea of the havoc they would wreak on this part of Europe. The tension here in the Balkans has its roots in centuries of hatred... - 28.6.98*

> *The situation has been brewing for at least 15 years, and the 90% Albanian majority could finally tolerate no more Serbian persecution. - 17.7.98*

It was questioned whether we were biased for printing this correspondence, but no-one wrote to us justifying the Serbian actions.

In August I went to Kosova again. I flew from Manchester to Munich "sardine class", as Adrian Plass says. In the transit lounge I waited with other passengers to Belgrade, and felt the knot of fear in my stomach as I heard the Serbian language: we were getting nearer, and I wondered what awaited me in Serbia and Kosova. The connecting flight to Belgrade was more roomy and comfortable and afforded marvellous views over the Austrian Alps for those with a window seat.

Strangely, as it seemed to me, I was not searched at all at the airport, and passed quickly through to the exit. But I fell victim to a con man almost immediately. It worked like this. You land in Belgrade, where you've never been before; you do not speak Serbian; you cannot read the alphabet; you do not know the system for buying long-distance bus tickets, nor how much to expect to pay... and a "friendly" taxi-driver, all smiles, says, "Wait in the taxi, and I'll get your ticket." So you accept, pay him, and find out when you ask the passenger next to you on the bus that he has multiplied the fare many times and pocketed the cash. You feel a fool, humiliated.

Then there was a five-hour bus journey to Prishtinë, with a stop for food and two police checks en route. Finally, at night, I arrived. Here is what I found.

The War

The day I arrived, the Serbian offensive began against Anton Krasniqi's native village, and he had no news of his family. An "offensive" meant shelling and burning houses, destroying crops and driving out the inhabitants to hide in the forests or to flee wherever they could. The Serbs had totally destroyed Anton's sister-in-law's house.

We visited a distant relative of his to console him on the death of his brother. He was much in tears as he told us the story: the Serbs had killed twelve people in the village where his brother lived, doused the house with petrol, and burnt it down; three of the dead had been buried, the others had disappeared.

A student we visited had no news of the his mother, brother or sister.

A journalist with the *Sunday Times* told me, "I've spent today watching people's homes being burnt down."

The Police

We visited Fatmir Ibrahimi, a young man, eager and committed in his faith, stayed at his home for about four hours, and ate with the family. After dinner we went for a walk - the famous Balkan *corso* when huge numbers of the population come out for an evening stroll, to chat, flirt, philosophise or catch up on gossip. We mingled with the crowds, and I ambled up and down, my head bowed in thoughtful conversation with Fatmir. When I looked up I noticed that the crowds had vanished. "Why?" I asked. It was time for the police to come.

At about 9.30 pm a discussion began about how we should get back to Anton's house - a mere twenty or thirty minute walk. Fatmir's brother wanted to take us by car, as it was considered too unsafe to be out at that time in the evening - not because of *criminals* but because of the *police*, who might rob or shoot you. In the end we decided to walk, and Fatmir and his brother escorted us some of the way. The police did not trouble us, contenting themselves with stopping cars, and we got home without ado.

The next evening, we visited a lady from the church, whose husband had been beaten by five policemen five months previously, so severely that he still had the marks. Another of the pastor's kith and kin had had his face stabbed by the police.

The bus no longer ran to Albania, and I had to travel via Macedonia after my visit. I noticed the agitation of the young woman sitting next to me as we approached one of the police checks on the road. People were living in fear. She also asked me about my faith, and said she would like me to send her some Evangelical literature. It took 1½ hours to cross the border, then the bus took us to Skopje.

The Atmosphere

The strange thing was that in Prishtinë life went on as normal. One saw police walking home after duty in camouflage uniform with Kalashnikoffs; armoured Land-Rovers marked TV; a line of Red Cross vehicles drawn up waiting to collect the wounded. And, so odd for the Balkans, one heard no music. But the day to day business of living went on seemingly as normal.

But under the surface there was suffering and fear everywhere. Anton reckoned the gunfire in the background as we walked home one evening was Serbs shooting to create an atmosphere of fear. The next evening, it was probably in celebration of their sporting victory over Russia. But the thing is, nobody ever knew:

it *could* be that the war had come to Prishtinë. They just never knew.

And oppression. One of the sisters in the church had been unemployed for ten years - sacked along with the other Albanians simply for being Albanian.

The Church

I asked Anton how many believers there were in Kosova, and he said maybe five hundred. I could not help wondering whether his estimate was rather optimistic. I also asked what the church's greatest need was at the moment. He said "Unity," and I must admit with sadness that the Lord's work was very fragmented and disunited, with little fellowship or cooperation between the churches in various towns, or even in the same town.

I asked Simo Ralević the same question, and his reply was: "Peace in Kosovo." I was unable to visit him because of the war, and there was no direct traffic going his town. We spoke over the phone. We also received a letter from him about that time:

> *Thank you for your kind letter. Things are being changing for worse so quickly that we are amazed. We have so many problems in the work that you will not believe. So we look to God for defending and protecting us. Orthodox Church, with all institutions of government, are creating atmosphere to forbid all Protestant work in Serbia. They are attacking us in news and tv almost every day.*

Anton was very isolated. The only two men of spiritual stature in his church were a good deal younger than he. He seemed pleased to be able to pray with me, and to ask my opinion on various matters: how should he handle his intense desire to speak out against the injustices of life in Kosova? how should he relate to people who have wronged him, damaged his work, and shown no iota of remorse? should he split his small congregation into two, and hold some services in Albanian and others in Serbian?

Not all pastoral problems are directly spiritual. There was the sister we visited whose husband left on a business trip six years previously and had never been seen since. Was he dead or alive?

Anton invited me to preach on the Sunday morning, and I opened the scriptures to the people on the theme of prayer. Anton added an extemporary peroration, and then there was a time of prayer in which several took part.

Literature

It was illegal to bring any Christian literature into Kosova. A few copies got in in people's pockets or carrier bags, but that was all. I was disappointed nonetheless that there was so little AEM literature at the church in Prishtinë, till I was told that this was because it was so popular that it disappeared quickly when it was brought.

Once literature was there it was possible to ensure it got to churches in other towns too. And in Prishtinë the Roman Catholic priest Nosh Gjolaj had it in his church library.

We got quotes from four printers, and planned to start printing there, which would make widespread distribution legal.

Throughout August Serbs and Albanians were killed in a series of attacks by the Kosova Liberation Army (KLA) and savage reprisals by the Serbs whose methods included "the horrific evidence of mass murder... massacred bodies of children - backs arched and mouths stretched open in terror. Some were shot in the back of the head. Others have throats cut or mutilated limbs. The killers slit the throat of one 10-year-old boy, blew out his mother's brains, cut open the stomach of another female relative and shot a pregnant woman in the head" (see *The Independent* 30th. September 1998).

The massacre which made war inevitable came in January 1999. On the 15th. day of the month, on a hilltop above the village of Raçak, forty-five people, including three women, a boy and many men over the age of 60, were shot and hacked to death by Serbian police and paramilitaries. The hilltop was then mined. A schoolteacher was the first to come afterwards to the site of the killings. She found corpses with no eyeballs or no arms, and body parts lying around on the ground. "I prayed to God," she said, "that their blood would become a guiding light to show Europe - to show Europe the truth."

The international community was appalled. The head of the Organisation for Security and Co-operation in Europe (OSCE), William Walker, spoke out against the slaughter.

Several monitors working for OSCE's Kosovo Verification Mission were beaten up by Serb forces.

The conflict spiralled out of control. The KLA increased its attacks on Serb police. The Serbs reluctantly attended a peace conference in Rambouillet, near Paris, beginning on the first weekend of February. President Milošević did not even come. The talks lasted three weeks, but Belgrade refused to allow a NATO force into Kosova and to permit a referendum on Kosova's future after a three-year interim government.

In February I received a letter from Anton Krasniqi:

We are well, despite all that is happening around us. Truly, we are grateful to God for His protection and every promise which, through Christ, is Yea and Amen... I want to thank you warmly for everything, beginning with the books we spoke of... and above all for the sincere friendship... Impatiently I await your coming...

The British public was becoming aware via television and newspaper reports of the troubles in Kosova, and one wondered how long the disturbances would go on and what they would lead to. The native population was 90% Albanian, but the Serbs held the guns and ran the police. A friend in neighbouring Macedonia told me that the violence was worse than shown on television. People were left dead in the streets.

I arrived in Prishtinë on 11th. March, in order to visit Anton and to arrange for the printing of a further three of AEM's titles. I travelled by bus from Skopje, and had a bottle of water with me to slake the dryness of my throat as we neared the border. I was tense. I had computer disks containing Albanian literature in my luggage and on my person, and I did not want to share the experience of the OSCE observers who had been harassed and beaten. The passengers were told to get off the bus and place our luggage on the pavement. Hollow and hidden places in the bus's interior were then searched for guns. Meanwhile outside, when the officials reached me, I was taken to an office, and a telephone call was made in Serbian; then I was allowed to continue my journey with no search.

The Serbs were trying to present their murder and thuggery as a war to cleanse Kosova of Islam, a glorious attempt to spread Christianity by driving out the Moslem Albanians and replacing them with Orthodox Serbs. When they burnt down an Albanian's house, they often painted the sign of the Cross and scrawled *With faith in God and in the name of Serbia* on the wall. The effect, of course, was to drive the Kosovars further into the arms of Islam, and to confuse them as to what Christianity really is. People were feeling their need of God, but it was the mosques that were full.

There were some fifty thousand internally displaced persons in Prishtinë. The Serbs provided no accommodation for them, and many were living in cramped conditions in the homes of local people, sometimes twenty to a room. Anton's new neighbours were such, and we spent an evening with them: they and their relatives had already seen five houses burnt down.

The Lord's people were attempting to provide aid, and were reaching about five hundred. The congregation at Anton's church had doubled since my August visit, and though some may have been drawn by the prospect of aid, they were coming under the sound of the Gospel and into contact with Christian people. Anton's nephew Artur had been helping to get aid to places beyond Prishtinë. One day he was with a Swiss aid lorry. The Serbs stopped it, put a gun to his throat and questioned him. It was the worst day of his life, and he was very grateful to be still alive.

I preached twice: at the Thursday meeting, and at the Sunday morning service. The former had to be held at 4pm, for it was too risky to be out in the evening, for fear of explosions, kidnap or police beatings. The congregation numbered about twenty.

Being British made me especially welcome, as Britain was seen as a country willing to do what it could to help the Albanians in their plight. I was warmly thanked for coming at a time of civil war and disruption, and for arranging for the printing of Christian literature in the province. The people appreciated knowing that they were held in our hearts.

On the Saturday evening we decided not to visit members of the congregation, because of reports of explosions in the town. The following morning - Sunday, 14th. - I preached to about two dozen people. I left that afternoon, and set off for Skopje and then Albania. By the Thursday as we approached Pogradec, it was snowing heavily, and I suspected that if the weather were similar in Kosova, it would no doubt give the Serbs an orgy of Schadenfreude over the many homeless Albanians whose houses they had wantonly destroyed.

On 19th. March the OSCE cease-fire monitors, who were unarmed civilians, were withdrawn from the province. The next day the Serb army began a major new offensive against Albanian positions. NATO intelligence officer Col. Bill Fillman commented: "We saw clear indicators that large-scale military operations against Kosovo were about to take place."

On Monday, 22nd. March Richard Holbrooke, the United States special envoy to the Balkans, together with his team, delivered an ultimatum to President Milošević in Belgrade: he must sign the agreement presented to him, or bombing would start. He refused.

Two hours after sunset on the Wednesday 24th. March, NATO launched its attack. More than fifty cruise missiles headed for Serbia and Kosova from American warships and a British submarine. They were followed by eighty war planes. My relief driver Paul Troon and I were still on our way home and that evening we reached Calais, and there we drew the day to a close with prayer, especially for Kosova.

The war which began that evening lasted eighty days.

The Serb forces stepped up their vicious rampage as soon as the NATO action began. The War Crimes Tribunal at the Hague claims that a mass killing took place on 25th. March 1999 at Krusha e Madhe. Residents took refuge in the forest and watched their houses burnt, but the police found them the following morning. The men were driven into a nearby house, and the Serbs opened fire. They then piled hay on the bodies and set fire to it. The war crimes charge sheet says that about a hundred and five men and boys were killed.

Two days later in Izbica Serb forces surrounded several thousand villagers taking refuge in a meadow outside the village, and killed about a hundred and thirty of them. Days later Serb police were said to have shot nineteen women and children in Gjakovë.

The Times' front page headline of 27th. March read "Serbs on murder spree: twenty villagers shot against school wall". The article said the Serbs "have gone on a bloody rampage against Albanians in Kosovo, murdering scores of civilians, using entire communities as human shields, and forcing thousands from their homes in an orgy of looting and burning." It was their final push for the ethnic cleansing of Kosova, to drive out 90% of its native population: the *Endlösung* that should fulfil the ancient Serbian dream.

During the next three months or so, according to British estimates reported in *The Times* in June, the Serbs killed ten thousand Albanians. The report added that Geoff Hoon, a Foreign Office minister, regarded the Serbs as "responsible for savagery that beggars belief". How could human beings be capable of "murdering children, systematic rape of young women and girls, digging mass graves and burning bodies to try to conceal the evidence of murder"?

On 9th. July Italian troops identified a mass grave at Ljubenic, thought to hold three hundred and fifty corpses. Nearby were thirty to forty charred bodies in a burnt-out house. *The Times* reported that most mass graves had been "robbed", that is, there was a co-ordinated plan to destroy bodies, which accelerated as Serb forces prepared to withdraw. They dug up lorry-loads of corpses, took them to steel-mills, foundries and mines to be dropped down shafts, incinerated in smelting plants or rendered down in vats of acid. On my November 1999 visit I was introduced to Josef Martinsen, a worker with Action by Churches Together, whose expertise was discovering human and animal bodies dumped along with garbage into wells and reservoirs, devastating Kosova's water supply.

According to Scripture:

> *Death as the completion and fulfilment of life is dependent upon decent and proper burial... In Israel this is deeply related to kin and land. Nothing is a worse outrage, offensive to God and man, than that a corpse should be left unburied, 'with the burial of an ass', as Jeremiah said of Jehoiakim (Jeremiah 22.10).*[2]

The systematic campaign to drive the Albanians out of the province continued. Towards the end of March, 65,000 people had already been driven from their homes. On 31st. March, an estimated 100,000 people were driven out of Prishtinë alone. On 1st. April about 10,000 refugees were forced at gunpoint to walk along the railway track to the border with Macedonia.

Among those who left were Anton and his family. A grenade had recently been thrown into the Serb café next-door to the church. The police were beating people up in the street outside the church, and he felt it was time to take his wife, three young children and widowed mother

---

[2] James Barr, *The Garden of Eden and the Hope of Immortality* (London, 1992)

to safety. They were taken to the border by a neighbour who was a Serb official, and who escorted them through the check-points to the Macedonian border as an act of friendship. May the Lord reward him! They then spent three days in no man's land and found a temporary lodging in the basement of the Evangelical Church in Skopje, before gaining a visa to go to Germany.

Anton's brother, a pastor in Gjakovë, escaped to Albania; Fatmir to Macedonia.

The printer who was printing our literature was driven from his home when Serbian forces came to his part of the town with machine guns and an axe and ordered the residents to gather some belongings and leave. He and his family spent a while in Macedonia, and were then admitted to Britain, where they went first to Runcorn and then to London.

In May we printed a report from Geoff Townsend of Gjirokastër, Albania:

Endless numbers of men have been shot down in front of their wives and families, with reports of the women being sexually abused. Think of their mental torture! of how their hearts are bleeding with the pains of injustice, hatred and barbaric cruelty! People are forced out of their homes in the middle of the night, everything taken from them, money, documents, car number plates, anything that identifies them as residents of Kosovo. The genocidal cleansing is escalating and we fear that it will not stop until the last is either killed or driven out.

How does this affect us in Albania? Homeless people, without food, without clothing, without money, full of desperation. The North of Albania overflowing, teaming

70

with refugees. They are being diverted to other towns in an overflow situation. Crisis centres are being set up throughout the country. I have had discussions with the other Christian groups in Gjirokastër and we are seeking to co-operate with the Mayor to co-ordinate the efforts to meet emergency needs in this town. We needed a co-ordinator and organiser. I have been given this task.

Mike and Judy Smith in Elbasan reported that Elbasan had received eleven thousand Kosovar refugees, and became heavily involved in caring for them. David and Pauline Wilcox, also in Elbasan, had twelve refugees living with them in their house, as well as being involved with feeding six hundred in the town and arranging accommodation for others.

Mike Brown in Korçë was appointed treasurer for the funds that came for refugee care via the evangelical churches of the town. "Frankly, we need as much as we can lay our hands on," he wrote. "There are massive needs... There are several thousand more on their way from Kukës."

Margaret Reid in Bilisht asked for financial help in her care for refugees.

The chapel in Ersekë looked more like a refugee camp than a place of worship, and the town asked the church to help with the feeding of all the refugees there. One man said his life was saved when the Serbs ran out of ammunition as they lined up all the people of his village and machine-gunned them.

Most churches in Albania suspended their normal programmes and focused almost entirely on refugee work.

In July 1999 we published the following reports from some of our missionaries:

Gjirokastër

from Alison Smith

By mid-April 2,400 refugees had arrived in the district, 1,500 of them in Gjirokastër itself. At first they were all put in the sports hall. The evangelical community has refurbished a largely disused metal factory, whose director and maintenance man offered it to house refugees. Preparing it was a major task.

from Geoff and Shirley Townsend

The work amongst the refugees is stabilising. We are getting ourselves more organised. Alison Smith has taken on the responsibility of managing the warehouse, with all of us helping by taking a day each when we are working, to free her up a bit. Shaun Thompson is doing distribution of food to various centres in Gjirokastër every Tuesday. At the beginning of July Shirley will be committing herself to being at the Shelter every morning to take care of the many little problems that are presently coming to Geoff. This will free him to get on with the bigger jobs.

We are having good opportunities to share the Word of God. Some are much more interested than others. We have been going to have coffee or tea with the different families and find this a good, natural way to share something of our faith. We are all building friendships and are praying for open hearts.

Penny Munden is involved in a meeting for pre-school children every Thursday morning and has been doing something for the older children on a Saturday afternoon. We are hoping for the privilege of holding a meeting for the adults soon on a Sunday afternoon. We have been moving cautiously and did not want to put on too much pressure.

Everyone at the Kosovars' Shelter is doing well, although they are struggling to cope with the heat. We too are finding that the heat is really sapping our strength. Two women are waiting daily for their babies to be born. Neither of them have heard whether or not their husbands are still alive. Many others have family members missing. We find it emotionally tiring to listen to all this, and feel helpless to do anything. We give God's comfort when we can.

A team from Wales came to do practical work, and brought about a transformation to the site in the old factory. The men piped water into all the toilets as well as fixed or built doors to enclose them and provide privacy. Most doors were falling off the hinges or missing. They put sinks into the bathrooms as well as installing showers, piping water into the showers and putting up shower curtains. They also put up hooks for clothes, and clothes lines to dry laundry, as well as building tables and benches for the dining room. Their last project was building Albanian baby cots! There are several pregnant women and the cots are very important.

Please pray for these people and for us as we come alongside them. One of the women has spoken to Shirley several times... They lived in a village and were forced to leave. Her father and brothers and their families remained blocked in in Prizren. Later, she heard that all Albanians had been given 30 minutes to leave the town. Now she has no idea if they are still alive, walking to get to Albania... There are no words to alleviate the pain. We want to share the comfort of the Lord with them, but are allowing them to talk and grieve before talking about the Lord. They do know that we are Christians, so we pray for natural open doors. Some have asked for Bibles, and one Sunday we had a small party for the children hosted by Dr. Mair Williams and John Thomas from South Wales. They got the children singing songs and John told the story of the Prodigal Son. There was a good response. We had lunch with them that day and it was good to receive hospitality from them and relax together.

Elbasan

from Mike and Judy Smith

We are providing for eight Kosova families. Our "Kosova N° 7" home is a house in a village on the outskirts of Elbasan. It was unfurnished and situated at the end of a lane barely wide enough to take our van. We had a job moving the furniture, especially as a neighbour had two loads of manure dumped between our van and the house whilst we were doing so. Fortunately two of our young Kosovars moved furniture and fixed electrics for us. The family came over from the tented camp in Durrës.

"Kosova N° 8", which is a flat, has been occupied by a family including a young woman who gave birth to a baby girl. When Judy visited this young mother in the maternity hospital she met three other mothers from one of the camps here. They cannot return to the camps as it is far too hot in the tents for the babies. They just wait for some better place to be found for them.

We opened a nursery class for the Kosovar children in a room which we have rented nearby. It is run by one of our Kosovars who is a trained teacher. It will take twenty children eventually. One of the little girls attending fell from her father's arms when he was killed by the Serbs as they were fleeing from Kosova - and so these horror stories keep on being poured out as time goes on. They need to talk and we to listen. We also opened a second nursery in another area of Elbasan which is situated in an existing state nursery building.

Berat

from Tony and Liz Treasure

There are not any words I can add to describe the evil which has swept Kosova.

No one is sure, but there are about 5000 refugees spread out in Berat in various venues, some better than others but basically derelict factories or empty schools. Many are without mattresses or adequate taps or toilets. Many with no lights etc. etc.

The stories we hear of the Serb brutality are beyond belief, and the suffering unimaginable. Everywhere are widows with their children.

We visit one family unit where almost all the menfolk were wiped out when the Serbs rounded up a hundred men and burnt them alive with only a handful surviving.

I [Liz] have become involved with several women who have recently given birth. We rented a wee flat and it was full with four women and babies. I visited each morning and helped with the health problems and general running of house, having three Albanian women working there so there is always someone about. This kept the babies out of the camps where the health risks to newborns are immense. The four women are a microcosm of the suffering here. One widow with no family to go to. One delivered on the back of a moving tractor heading out of Kosova, looking back to see her home burning and her husband who was taken and almost certainly killed with the other men. One was in an antenatal ward when the Serbs came and ordered them out. She fled with her uncle's family and finally ended up in Berat where she gave birth to a wee boy. But her husband and other two children were in another town so she has no news of them.

All day on TV here they flash names across hoping to reunite families, name after name and where they are. One traumatised woman, raped, heard she has lost thirty members of her family.

Ersekë

from Dan Baynes

The powderkeg explodes

The Balkans have long been known as the tinderbox of Europe, and the province of Kosovo to the north-east of Albania proper has stood out as the most volatile area of all.

Imagine 4 million people flooding into Britain in a week. That, to scale, is what has happened to Albania; and the situation in the Republic of Macedonia is hardly better.

I'd like to give you a few glimpses of what various individuals associated with me have been and are doing to help alleviate a crisis 'of Biblical proportions' (as they say).

Until the end of March, we at AEM in the south had not yet felt the tremors rumbling down from the northern border with Kosovo - but we sure knew they were coming.

When April was an hour old, fifty refugees arrived in Ersekë, being put up at our church centre. Viola and I did not see them, as we decided to make our way back to Tirana via Korçë, where we spent time with Mike and Suela Brown. That afternoon we helped prepare forty or fifty packets with nappies and other materials suitable for nursing mothers, which with a pile of loaves of bread we took up the hill to the usually empty building used as a retreat by workers in Communist times. I understand that that building at that time held about 170 refugees, with about 500 in the town overall.

On the Saturday Viola and I were going to make a quick start for Tirana, but in view of the crisis she spent that morning preparing lunch for about 200 refugees - reputedly the first hot meal they'd have had in a week. Well, actually a lot of other work had to be done first: this was in a school adjoining a property run by Kolping which needed a lot of floor-cleaning. So out came the brooms and sponge-tipped sweepers - for although one room had taps there was no drainage system, so we simply flushed it all out of the door in among the pile of old desks that had been hastily removed from the building. Then came all the potato-chopping etc., and cooking with a gas stove as the place had no electric plug.

I said earlier that fifty Kosovars came to Ersekë on April 1st.; four days later there were 170 there, and of course many public buildings and homes as well as the church have had to be opened for them. Actually when they were first brought there, the Kosovars, on seeing the cross atop the Orthodox church next to the Evangelical, thought they'd been taken south right into pro-Serbian Greece or even worse Serbia itself, and had to be compelled by police to disembark! They did not have a good first impression of Korçë either, with its great big Orthodox cathedral in a prominent place, Greek folk music being played in public, and other culturally unsettling or alien trappings.

Back in Ersekë I aimed to make myself useful in whatever simple work was on, particularly on the catering side, and especially slicing bread, bread, bread... imagine nine or ten crates each with eight loaves sliced into twenty, for three meals a day. One soon learned not to attempt it on loaves fresh from the baker's oven!

Korçë

We were snowed in under an avalanche of refugees. The city's infrastructure was completely weighed down by it all, and we have been stretched beyond our limits. Mike Brown has been appointed treasurer for the funds that come in via the evangelical churches. The evangelical community signed a contract with the local government to take responsibility for the transit centre, which meant they could minister to every Kosovar who came into Korçë, providing something warm to eat and drink, and an open ear to listen to their stories, plus basic sanitary and hygienic needs.

Bilisht

from Margaret Reid

Over 2000 refugees arrived, with no food, shelter or change of clothing. The small evangelical fellowship offered them transit accommodation, followed by regular visits taking bedding, food, clothing, medical care &c.. The task of trying to meet their needs has been enormous, but has given opportunity also to talk about the Lord and to pray with them. Some are open to spiritual things, and a few have come regularly to the church in Bilisht or the women's meetings in Bitinckë. Two have professed faith.

Thank you for the gifts you sent for the Kosovar refugees. The money we received was spent firstly on emergency items for the 600 refugees located in three places where local believers could handle the distribution. Later on we were able to take on the weekly buying and distribution of fresh vegetables and eggs to the entire 1,700 refugees in the district of Devoll.

When NATO forces eventually moved through Kosova they uncovered evidence of horrific killings. One of their most shocking discoveries was the torture chamber at the police station in Prishtinë, with its array of knuckle dusters, truncheons, cudgels, a 2-foot knife, baseball bat, chains, pickaxe, car battery for electrode treatment, black hood; and the bed. The bed had a leather strap for restraining victims, and a bullet-ridden mattress.

A report in *The Times* said that Serb forces laid at least 616 mine fields containing tens of thousands of anti-personnel devices, which were still, at the end of August, killing up to five people a day.

The International War Crimes Tribunal in the Hague accused Milošević and four other Serbian leaders of crimes against humanity, including responsibility for the murder of hundreds of civilians and the deportation of 740,000 Albanians. *The Independent* reported that almost a million had been deported. The European Union said it would cost £650 million per year for three years to rebuild Kosova after the destruction that had been wrought during the war. The *Frankfurter Allgemeine Zeitung* (19.11.99) reported that the European Commission and the World Bank estimated the need for re-building Kosova in the coming four to five years at around 2.4 thousand million dollars: re-building or repairing more than 100,000 houses and restoring the infrastructure.

Such was the outworking of the Serbs' drive to cleanse Kosova of most of its native population.

Chapter 8: A Door set open

The Lord your God has set the land before you.

- Deuteronomy 1:21

The Serbian army withdrew and the NATO forces entered Kosova on Saturday, 16th. June, but the Serbs had managed to get a significant concession from NATO: the promise of a referendum on independence was revoked, and it was agreed that Kosova would remain within Yugoslavia. One cannot help fearing that that concession sowed the seeds for future bloodshed and war. One thing is certain: the future is unknown.

In the weeks after the Serb surrender, Serbs began to flee from Kosova. The Serb population there before the war was about 180,000; by mid-July it was down to less than 50,000. On 29th. June *The Guardian* reported a Red Cross estimate that fewer than 25,000 Serbs remained in Kosova. *The Times* reported on 31st. August that the number of Serbs in Prishtinë was down from 40,000 to less than 2,000 in just a few months.

By January 2000, when ITV screened Jonathan Dimbleby's report of his journey to Kosova, there were only a thousand Serbs remaining in Prishtinë, and 75% of the Serbian population had left the province - some 150,000 people. It was no longer possible for the two communities to live together in peace.

The now dominant Albanian population - or certain elements among them - began sustained intimidation of the remaining Serbian population. More than seventy of their churches were desecrated or destroyed. It was reported in the *Daily Mail* of 19th. June that soldiers of the KLA burst into the Serbian Orthodox monastery at Devic. The bell was being rung for Sunday prayers for the priest and nine nuns, a week earlier. The youngest nun was 24 years old. The KLA soldiers ordered her to strip. "No," she screamed. The priest, who tried to shield her, was punched, kicked and beaten with a rifle butt. The soldiers lost interest and the nun was not defiled; but the incident shows that there were evil men on both sides: all are fallen, Albanian and Serb. Five days later the local KLA commander arrived at the monastery. "If what I have heard is true, I will say sorry."

The Independent (29 June) reported that "only a handful joined the Serbian Orthodox Patriarch to mark the 610th. anniversary of the Battle of Kosovo Polje." According to *The Guardian* there were half a dozen priests, one local policeman and not a single ordinary civilian.

The warehouse and office outside Pejë, where Simo Ralević stored Christian literature, was burnt down on 14th. June. The warehouse contained literature in four languages, and it was all destroyed except for twenty Albanian titles. He also lost a third of his personal library at his home in the town. His church was used by a Pentecostal fellowship, and he and his family removed to Vojvodina.

The same week as the KLA appeared at the monastery at Devic, evidence emerged that they had begun to torture suspected informers: German Kfor troops released fifteen badly beaten prisoners, but were too late to save the sixteenth, a 70-year-old man hand-cuffed dead to a chair.

That autumn we published these reports:

From Margaret Reid, July 1999

Thank you for being with us in prayer. Today nine Albanians from the village of Bitinckë set off to take part in the rebuilding of Kosovar homes and to continue the building of relationships with our Kosovar friends. Four of these nine are Christians. The two young people, Alketa and Kleanti, are by far the most mature Christians, whereas the two older men are still pretty young in their faith.

For many years people have prayed that one day Albanians would become missionaries to their own people in Balkan countries. This is now becoming a reality as believers like Alketa go to Kosova with the primary desire of sharing Christ with the Kosovar people. Kosova is over 90% Muslim and the people are much more religion-conscious than in Albania.

On Sunday 18th July Steve Galegor, Pastor of the Korçë Church, Arjan Larashi, Pastor of the Bilisht fellowship, Koseta from Bilisht and I will go to Kosova for a couple of days to meet the families we were closest to and to assess the damage to their properties. It may be some time before a building team can be placed in their area but we feel that a visit is timely to show that we continue to be interested in them and concerned to help them. It is reported that their homes are completely destroyed.

From Margaret Reid, August, 1999

I just got back from two weeks in the villages north of Prishtinë where the building team from Bitinckë and Korçë is working. This is a joint project with World Relief. Altogether they have taken on 100 homes and are aiming to have them made weatherproof by mid-October.

Alketa continues to serve them (15 for breakfast and dinner, 20+ for lunch every day) with cheerfulness and a true sense of being in the place God wants her. Please pray for her. There are two other Albanian volunteers whom the Lord is using daily to speak for him with the Kosovar people. Until the beginning of September a Korçë pastor, Aliu, was on site and he was leading daily devotions with the team and available to minister wherever needed, whether to Albanian workers or Kosovars.

It's almost impossible to find a moment alone because of cramped living conditions and the fact that Kosovars like to be with people all the time. One day as I went in search of my Bible, I found one of the volunteers using it to tell the story of creation and the fall to a lady from the village. After a while they moved on and left me reading when along came a man called Naim, who asked what the book was about. I let him read it for himself and he liked what he read. "This book gives life." A small group of us visited his family a couple of nights later in their tent and over many glasses of sweet Russian tea enjoyed sharing more of God's word with him. This man and his sister Ferdie are probably the most spiritually open people I've met so far in Kosova.

They came into Prishtinë with us on the Sunday to a church service.

From Margaret Reid, September, 1999

First of all the very good news that Ferdia has come to faith in Christ. One day Alketa's father Skender could not work on the buildings because of a painful nerve in his leg. So he went to the morning devotions time to ask for prayer. It happened that Ferdia went along that day to listen... Skender told the story of how the Lord had worked in his family and how he, his wife and Alketa came to know Christ. Ferdia went away by herself, found a quiet corner and gave her life to Christ. Please pray for her. She is avidly reading all the Christian material she can lay her hands on.

The team have now left her village, Samadrexh, and have moved about ten kilometres down the road to another village, so that leaves her a lone believer. Her brother Naim continues to be spiritually open.

I am planning to go back to Kosova with Alketa on the 16th of September because the village the team is now working in is the place where my closest contacts live. Please will you pray for the development of our personal relationships to be loving and for the Lord to open their minds and hearts to seek him.

The main town in the area where our team is working is called Vushtri. As far as we can tell there is no Christian witness at all in that town. We did not have any contacts to follow up there, but while in Samadrexh a man came to us and asked if we could help his sister-in-law. This lady's husband had been a commander in the Kosova Liberation Army. One day she and her children were sitting down to a meal when there was a knock at the door and someone came in and presented her husband's head on a plate and laid it on the table. She is still in a state of shock. At the moment she is doing the rounds of family staying in a different place for a few days. Although we had actually reached our quota of homes to take on, we feel that we should do all we can to help this woman.

Once the building team returns to Albania in the winter we are proposing to continue regular visits, maybe monthly, to this area of Kosova in order to continue the gospel witness initiated and to show that our interest is genuine.

After Margaret's last visit in September she felt she did not want to see Kosova again for a long time. There had been relationship problems between the building team and Kosovars once they moved to Milosheva. Many of the things that happened were not a good witness and Margaret came back to Albania exhausted and depressed, and feeling that on a spiritual level Kosova is a very difficult place to work. There is a heaviness that is hard to penetrate.

Alketa, who worked alongside the building team supplying meals, was considering returning to Kosova to work with a programme helping war widows run by World Relief with whom they had worked in the house rebuilding programme.

From Geoff Townsend:

On Saturday 10th. July Geoff Townsend and Andrew Geuter set of for Suharekë, Rahovec and the Prizren area, where the refugees they had cared for in Gjirokastër had returned home. Their purpose was to assess the needs so as to form a clearer picture of how to continue to help them. As well as the damage wrought by the Serbs on property, they came across heart-rending stories. It was their desire to show love both in words and also in action and truth.

Geoff wrote:

Suharekë was the first town that we visited. All of the Serbian population have fled. Water is a problem at the moment. Most people have their own supply by drilling on their properties. [There is] a question as to what extent the homes are damaged structurally. The town stands void of actively operated shops where there was once a thriving shopping centre.

One shop displayed walls peppered with shrapnel, 40+ people were placed inside and then a grenade thrown in. Sad, heart-wrenching stories of massacres on a large scale. A family sits in a field lost and bewildered in deep and painful mourning of the 17 people in their family that were massacred. We went to pay our respects to them sitting with them. How can we feel the depth of their pain, their deep grief, their loss? You try to tell them not to take revenge, for that is for God alone: He will avenge, He alone is the righteous judge of men.

We moved on to Reshtan, a village of 200 families. Almost all of their homes are damaged in varying degrees. We sat on the floor on the thin pieces of sponge that the refugees had whilst they were in Gjirokastër. If it were not for these items that they brought back with them they would be like many others with hardly anything. Food is becoming more readily available, although humanitarian aid organisations are not yet as effective as needed to be. I say this not as a criticism but as an observation of the mammoth task that looms over them.

Heavy rains have fallen recently, which started to cause them great problems. The rooms that are being used for collective sleeping are very damp. Their roof no longer exists so all the rain is being soaked up into the walls. The bedding felt damp as we sat on it. Much needs to be done and as quickly as possible because of the cold weather that sets in very quickly around the middle of October. Temperatures drop drastically and can go as low as -22°F. The snows can reach a depth of three feet. People we have met are ready to do the repairs but have lost almost everything and most have no work to earn money. Factories standing idle, farm equipment stolen, damaged or destroyed to stop them working the land. Areas of farmland cordoned off for fear of land mines.

In another area we visited, one family of six people have been reduced to living in a very small outhouse in their yard. The parents sleep along with their eldest son, 20, their daughter, 18, plus the two younger boys. While we were there enjoying their warm hospitality despite the lack of facilities we were also joined by a rat scampering along the beams.

Many people have acknowledged God's saving hand in their situations. I must say that I have learnt to trust some of these people greatly and have a great respect for their moral standards even though they may be unregenerate. It appears that some who are practising

Muslims are close to the Kingdom of God according to the conversations that we have had with them.

In September, Geoff made his fourth trip to Kosova. This trip differed from the previous ones in that his wife Shirley went with him. She appears earlier in this book as Shirley Klippenstein, and it was a return trip for her after an eight-year span of service in Albania. Shirley had looked forward eagerly to visiting Kosova, but had been disappointed on other occasions when Geoff went and she had had to stay in Gjirokastër for security reasons at their home.

This trip involved bringing two more lorries of aid that still remained in the warehouse in Gjirokastër - that which had not been stolen from them. They had been paying three guards to watch over the warehouse yet they arrived on site and found the front entrance locked from the inside and had to force their way in, only to find yet another mess and further losses. Lorries were found and loaded, documents completed. From start to the finish it was one massive headache fraught with difficulties and stresses. Geoff explains:

Lorries complete with drivers found, their word given, great! teams of volunteers to load arranged, great! Aid in the warehouse sorted ready, great! Comes the day to load. Where is the driver who said, "Don't worry I will never let you down, you have my word! I have a family to feed and keep. Look at the calluses on my hands. I am not afraid of work"? Where was he with his word when we needed him?

We had loaded one lorry and the volunteers were still waiting to load the second one. I went to the driver's house but he had no intention of coming or even of letting us know that he would not keep his word.

Pressure from the driver who was already loaded to go and complete his documents, pressure from the volunteers waiting to load, stress from running around trying to secure a further lorry at short notice, all of these things together led to quite an exciting day.

Finally Shirley and I left for Kosovo via Macedonia. What an upset when the Macedonian police stopped Shirley from entering. Her passport was almost full and they required a full page for the entry visa as well as the return. Shirley was upset. I took her back into Albania and after composing ourselves she got onto a minibus for Elbasan; there she stayed for two nights. I travelled on into Kosovo alone arriving very late that evening.

Shirley was to come in [via a different border crossing, avoiding Macedonia] with one of the Kosovars who left from Suharekë especially to escort her in.

I went to the border crossing at Morina the following morning to meet the lorries coming with the aid. Problems! Problems! Our documentation had been incorrectly completed at the customs in Albania and what a headache this gave me when trying to leave Albania. Police and customs officials asking us to give them materials from the load, but I was having no part in their dirty work. I told one policeman that I understood what was happening and that he should not be so corrupt and that I would not give him anything as a bribe. They kept us waiting for 5 hours but eventually patience and grace won the day.

During their two-week stay Shirley and Geoff sorted and distributed the aid from Gjirokastër. Geoff continues the story:

> *Further stress and emotional pressure piled on. Jealousy and envy was seen in their fullness! Heart-wrenching emotional pressure when a decision is made to help one family and then the extended family or neighbours come and ask "Why can't you help me as well, or my sister, or brother?" To have to tell these that we cannot help everyone or that there are others in greater need than them is not easy.*

Geoff and Shirley hope to continue with the contacts they have and to build upon those relationships. They look forward to seeing those who have time for them for who they are, and not only for the material benefits they bring with them. Their hope is that such contacts will see the Lord with and in them.

Everywhere they had already worked they were known as the organisation that is helping people to build new homes. The Kosovars hold high hopes and expectations! Geoff and his colleagues have been able to assist about thirty-five families financially or materially.

He found that food aid was still scarcely getting into the hands of the people in the areas where he had been working and visiting. What they did receive was insufficient to sustain them even with basic supplies.

On his last day he visited a factory that previously employed up to 3,600 workers. Many had started back to work to try and build up the trade they previously had. They were doing so without any wage but just for the hope of a better future, and had mainly been eating quite meagrely at the factory. The director is related to the people Geoff stayed with each time he went there. He took half a ton of goulash, boxes of macaroni, a large quantity of tea, 100kg of sugar, seven hundred bars of soap, approximately a thousand toothbrushes and a quantity of toothpaste to the workers.

From Dan Baynes, July and August, 1999

By the time you get this most of the Albanians who came to Albania from Kosovo will have returned home (or to whatever is left of their homes), apparently heedless of danger from mines and violent conflict between the ethnicities there.

Ian Loring and Mark Stoscher of Ersekë have been running trips to Kosovo to keep up the contacts and set up further humanitarian effort.

Despite obvious differences, Kosovo '99 looks increasingly like Albania '91, most importantly in terms of a new ease of entry by foreigners. Under Serbian rule it had been difficult to get entry visas for Kosovo.

Now all this has changed, and one can expect (to use a perhaps slightly unkind phrase) a sort of 'evangelical gold rush' into Kosovo parallel to that which happened in the case of Albania eight years ago. For there is a class of persons who are definitely attracted by just the sort of challenge Kosovo now presents, which naturally includes a scope for a lot of material aid as well, just as in Albania before. May God open the way for a substantial new thrust into this invitingly beckoning mission frontier, and bless all its work therein.

Margaret Reid forwarded to us a report by the Evangelical Alliance in Albania:

> There are around 300 different agencies working in Kosova and nobody really knows what they are doing. THE WINTER WILL BE VERY DIFFICULT.
>
> There are some new developments regarding the situation in between the churches in Kosova. They are moving toward an understanding that they need to work together, they need an alliance. But they are realising that an alliance is a matter of hearts and not papers.
>
> I have to mention also that there are many zones not covered or not at all picked from any of the Christian groups working in Kosova. We have mentioned even before: Istog, Klina, Lipjan, Gjilan, Vushtri, etc. We would like to challenge you to pray for these places, so God can provide somebody there very soon.

In July 1999 I too made a further visit to Kosova. It was a pleasant coincidence (I prefer the term "providence") when a voice said to me at Heathrow airport at 5:45 am, "What are you doing here reading at this time of the day?" and there was Mike Brown flying via Rome to Thessalonica. I did not know he was flying back that day, but it gave us the opportunity for an evening together in Thessalonica - a dolefully lonely city, as huge cities tend to be. He caught the midnight bus to Albania, but I left him about 11:20 and went to bed at the nearby Rex Hotel.

The next day I was met at the railway station in Skopje by Geoff Townsend, who had come in his Land Rover from

Gjirokastër. We first collected a good deal of Albanian literature from a man with whom I had previously left it for onward passage to Kosova, and then went on to Kosova.

The family we visited that evening in Suharekë had been refugees in Gjirokastër under Geoff's care, and now he was following them up, plus some eighteen other families in the area, and helping rebuild their burnt and ruined homes. After my return we sent him £30,000 to help with that - from money which people around Britain had kindly sent to our Kosovar Fund.

The family consisted of twenty-eight souls - four brothers, a cousin, their wives and children. Their father had disappeared, and was presumed dead. Extensive inquiries had uncovered no trace of him. Of the three houses on their farm, only two rooms were left un-burnt. There was not even a toilet. Even the stable was burnt, and the tethered cattle inside burnt alive. And the tractor and harvester in the farmyard.

In the morning one of the farmers took me for a walk around the neighbourhood - house after house burnt and ruined. Apparently the Serbs used some kind of flame-thrower and a gas or liquid that ignites and gives a specially fierce fire. When Geoff first went, the smell of rotting corpses was everywhere, but now they had been buried and the smell had passed away. I was shown two graveyards with stakes bearing only numbers, no names: the victims were unknown, or unrecognisable.

In Prishtinë I could not visit my old friend Anton Krasniqi, as he had left and gone to Germany. My obvious first step was to go to his church building and manse to make contact with his nephew Dritan, whom I had informed of our coming and through whom I hoped to make further contact with the other pastors in Kosova. The church, house and yard were swarming with people, mainly foreign - glad Christian workers with Evangelical smiles, joy and buoyancy, eager to be a blessing to the Kosovars. I could not face mingling with such jolly magnanimity: where had they all been last year? So when an Albanian lady who knew me offered to take us to Fehmi Cakolli, pastor of another church in the town, I gladly accepted.

I had met Fehmi on my May 1997 visit. By now he was soon to get married to a young woman from the church in Prizren, Belkize Kryeziu. He had about 30 people in his church.

In Kosova there were currently six Protestant churches: four Pentecostal, and two non-charismatic. Anton's flock had been scattered, though a number worshipped with one or other of the other churches.

I gave Fehmi the books brought from Skopje; collected 1870 more from the printer's works - of the 4000 we had ordered to be printed in Prishtinë: the rest were lost during the war. And I gave him disks with five more books to take to the printer.

There were plenty of Moslem bookshops in Kosova, but not one Christian bookshop. Fehmi wanted to get one opened, and we discussed the possibility of AEM's being involved financially in getting it up and running. In early 2000 AEM sent him £5000 towards the first year's running costs, with the promise of further grants the following two years.

On the Monday of my visit there was a 9-hour power cut, not just in Prishtinë but throughout the whole of Kosova. We went to Maxhunaj, the village where my host's family had its house - now a burnt-out ruin. (My host was Rexhep, the brother of the man who had run the printing works before the war and was now in Britain.) In the evening, when we got back, we learnt that a Serbian woman had been shot outside his flat and the gunmen had driven off in a car: part of the intimidation against Serbs mentioned above.

On the Tuesday I was taken first to Vushtrri: more ruined houses, and a pile of rubble where the Serbs had demolished the mosque.

Then on to Mitrovicë, where Rexhep (an electrician by trade) wanted to give advice to a relative whose house had been burnt and who needed to rewire it. On the way he kept talking about a bridge which was dangerous to cross - bombed during the war, I supposed, but not as badly as the one we had seen near Prishtinë. The nearer we got, the more he talked about it. Then it became clear that the danger was not from war damage, but from Serbs. The river Ibar cuts the town in two, and north of it towards the Serbian border, Serbs are more in number than Albanians, and were armed. Some of the Serbs were living there before, others had settled after the war including police from areas where atrocities were committed, who had laid aside their uniforms and kept their guns. The French are perceived as pro-Serb, and they had not disarmed the people. *The Times* reported on 26th. June that French Kfor troops stood by while Serb vigilantes blocked the bridge barring entry to "their" side by Albanians. The Serb side had most food shops and the only hospital. French commanders argued that it was not up to them to ensure safe passage for civilians. Our car had a Prishtinë number-plate - a give-away that the driver was probably Albanian.

At the bridge the French stopped us, and made us get out of the car while they searched it. Then we crossed. I offered a silent prayer for protection while we were north of the river. When we arrived at the house, Rexhep's relative Bedri asked whether we had had any trouble. By 7:05, when we left the house, Rexhep considered it already too late to visit another relative that side of the river, and (the car being searched again) we crossed back to the Albanian side.

On all these visits I kept meeting people whose relatives had been killed or had disappeared, and being shown places where killings took place, where Serbian snipers hid and shot at people passing by, where men had been imprisoned, or where the dead bodies of cattle or humans had lain. It was difficult to know how to respond appropriately when Besim Rexhaj, who was taking Rexhep and me to a café for a cup of coffee and some conversation, told me as he drove along that six of his relatives had been killed in the recent conflict, of whom three had been burnt alive. Mainly I was not told of people's *own* sufferings. Maybe their own experiences were too painful for them to relate.

The views often reminded me of photographs of Berlin at the end of the War: ubiquitous destruction. But in a way it was worse than the damage after a war: usually, an army will destroy what stands in its way (barracks, armaments, factories...), but the Serbs went from house to house destroying the homes, livelihood, cattle, property and lives of innocent civilian people: grannies who wanted to spend their remaining months in quietness, beautiful girls on the threshold of womanhood whom they raped and traumatised, peace-loving farmers, fathers, brothers, breadwinners shot and left unburied.

What impressions did I bring back home? Many, of course, but maybe mostly:

- the admirable, unbroken spirit of these resilient people, who returned to the ruins of their homes and lives and began to clean up, rebuild and start all over again

- the sign of the Cross painted on burnt-out dwellings, a token of the Serbs' blasphemous conceit that they were doing God's work by driving out Moslems, and the Cyrillic characters around the Cross representing *samo sloga Srbiju spašava*: only unity will save Serbia.

The hatred and wrath of the Serbs was not extinguished by the war: understandable enough, but they were not averse to selecting innocent victims on whom to vent it. Towards the end of September, the KLA captured three Serbs. On 29th. September two missionaries living in Albania, Lee and Kathy Church, were travelling with an Albanian worker on the road east of Prizren in Kosova, when they encountered a roadblock. A crowd of angry Serbs stopped them, and the travellers were made to get out of the car. They were beaten, tied up, blindfolded, robbed and held captive for five hours. The Albanian worker needed hospitalisation, and it was not till a week after the event that the party were able to return to Albania: even then they needed assistance from Kfor to cross the border, as the Serbs had stolen their vehicle licence plates.

On 29th. October I set off in my Land-Rover with my colleague Trevor Baker for the final visit to Kosova in this book. We had on board, all in Albanian, three thousand copies of the Evangelical Press publication *Ultimate Questions*, more than thirteen hundred copies of J. J. Lucas's *The Death of Christ*, over seventy pieces of literature about creation supplied by Ian McNaughton of Coventry, four thousand calendars from the Trinitarian Bible Society (to be divided between Kosova and Albania, whither we went after Kosova).

We linked up with Fehmi Cakolli, who kindly invited me to preach on the Sunday morning (7th. November), when I opened to them the book of Job. Following the sermon, two of the congregation gave moving testimonies of the help that came from God during the recent war. One said her husband had been beaten to death; she herself was still limping after receiving a beating and a broken leg. The other, a young man called Astriti, had been weak from days without food and water and unable to reach the border to escape; he prayed for divine help and felt an assurance he would receive it the following morning. The next day, he woke to find a bag of food by his tent, and never knew where it came from. In the strength of it he managed to cross to safety.

I felt that the service was a time of rich, serious fellowship.

As in July, I stayed with Rexhep and his family, who are of course Moslems. On the last two evenings he turned the conversation to spiritual matters, and I attempted to answer his questions helpfully, and gave him two books. The day drew to a close by candlelight, because of yet another power cut.

The next morning Trevor and I left Kosova in mist and drizzle, taking the war-damaged road that leads from Ferizaj to Tetova in Macedonia. There were few border formalities, and the Polish soldier, seeing our British passports, brought our vehicle to the front of the queue when the traffic began to move towards the exit barrier. From there we headed for Albania and then home.

* * *

We have called this little book *We came to Kosova*. Such a phrase sometimes speaks in the Bible of a moment of crisis, of decision, of significance for the future, or of an opportunity to begin a new stage or undertaking in the Lord's service:

> *And we set out... and went through all that great and terrible wilderness which you saw... and **we came to Kadesh-barnea**.*

There God told Moses to send men to spy out the land He was giving them. They reported that it flowed with milk and honey, and displayed its fruit, and Caleb said, "Let us go up at once."

Or again:

> *The hand of our God was upon us, and he delivered us from the hand of the enemy and from ambushes by the way. **We came to Jerusalem**...*

These words from Ezra 8, so applicable by God's kindness to our own travels in Kosova and Albania, describe the journey of Ezra and his company which led into his time of teaching, enriching, leading, purifying and re-establishing God's people in their land after their sufferings, defeat and exile in Babylon.

And so with us: **we came to Kosova**. And what we saw, we have set before you in these pages.

The book began with 1973: Albania was closed, and Kosova had only Simo Ralević in Pejë as an Evangelical witness: no Albanian church, no foreign missionaries. Now both lands are open, and both have young churches.

But this is not a time to slacken our zeal or relax our efforts. Rather, with the new situation in Kosova, it is a time of crisis, decision, significance and opportunity; a time to press ahead, for the Lord has set before us an open door. Kosova lies open before us. We must, under God, grasp every opportunity offered by the new circumstances, and either go or (if God does not permit us) pray for others to go.

"And I heard the voice of the Lord saying, 'Whom shall I send, and who will go for us?' Then I said, 'Here am I! Send me.'"

We hope this little book will help to stir compassion and concern, and a vision for the spread and acceptance of the Gospel in Kosova, and that the desire of those who read it will be like Isaiah's desire who prayed, "Here am I! Send me."

If despite that good desire God has entrusted other work and a different call to us, let us fervently and persistently offer the prayer taught us by the Lord, "Pray therefore the Lord of the harvest to send out labourers into his harvest."

But to some His words may also come personally, "Behold, I send you." If so, go, and as you come to Kosova, may you be fruitful for the salvation and blessing of many Kosovars, and for the praise of your Lord, Jesus Christ.

The passage from Deuteronomy 1 concerning Kadesh-barnea, quoted above, continues:

And I said to you, "You have come to the hill country of the Amorites, which the Lord our God gives us. Behold, the Lord your God has set the land before you; go up, take possession, as the Lord, the God of your fathers, has told you; do not fear or be dismayed."